The Sculpture World of Jerry Harris

Suzanne Fredericq and Jerry Harris

ISBN: 978-0-9825704-1-8

Foreword

When I think of a Jerry Harris sculpture I see birds, wading birds, the most graceful of birds. With their long stilts and immobile poses they ponder whether to take flight or stay put. And most stay put, firmly grounded, preferring the earth to the heavens -- all the while dreaming of heavens.

When I think of a Jerry Harris sculpture I see wheels, spinning wheels, the most acrobatic of the flywheels. With their spinning and mobile poses they ponder whether to stay put or take flight. And most take flight, in a hurry, preferring the heavens to the earth -- all the while dreaming of the earth.

When I think of a Jerry Harris sculpture I see clay that begs to become bronze and bronze that begs to transform into wood. And then, from clay to bronze and from hardwood to softwood, these noble materials will be carved, assembled, disassembled, fired, molded, welded, cast -- all the wile satisfying both the heavens and the earth.

Suzanne Fredericq,

Lafayette, Louisiana, September 12, 2009

Jerry Harris (b. Pittsburgh, Pennsylvania, born November 23, 1945) is an African American abstract sculptor, collagist and writer. Harris is primarily a constructivist sculptor, working in media such as wood, stone, bronze, fiberglass, clay, metal, mixed media (found objects), and collage.

After graduating from high school in Pittsburgh, he spent a year in Portland, Oregon where he attended Community College, and subsequently transferred to Tuskegee Institute, Alabama, and San Francisco State University. Harris then studied sculpture under James Lee Hansen, a leading Pacific Northwest sculptor. Harris was later accepted in the international sculptor's program at the St Martins School of Art, now Central Saint Martins College of Art and Design London, England, were his teachers included Sir Anthony Caro, Phillip King and Frank Martin. He also did special studies in bronze casting at the former *The Central School of Art and Design*, London, under Henry Abercrombie.

Harris lived in Stockholm and Lund, Sweden, for many years until the death of his wife, the Swede Britt-Marie Olofsson-Harris in 1996. He befriended many African American visual artists while living in Sweden, such as Herbert Gentry and Harvey Cropper. In 1998 Harris returned to the United States and his hometown of Pittsburgh. He was elected into *The Associated Artists of Pittsburgh*, the nation's second oldest artists' association, where he felt welcomed by the African American sculptor Thaddeus Mosley. Harris later moved to Eugene, Oregon, and currently lives in Chico, California.

Since 1988 Harris is a member of the *Swedish Sculptors Association*. His sculptures can be found in many private national and international collections, and in the permanent Swedish National Art Collection in Stockholm (Statenskonstrad). He has exhibited throughout Sweden, Europe, and the United States in various galleries and museums.

http://www.harrisculptor.com/

http://www.youtube.com/user/sirepurdue
http://en.wikipedia.org/wiki/Jerry_Harris

This publication includes images of forty-seven sculptures created by sculptor Jerry Harris between the 1980's and 2009. The sculptures are made of carved and constructed wood, mixed media, iron, found objects, laminated clay (Bondo), or bronze.

Dedicated to Britt-Marie Olofsson-Harris

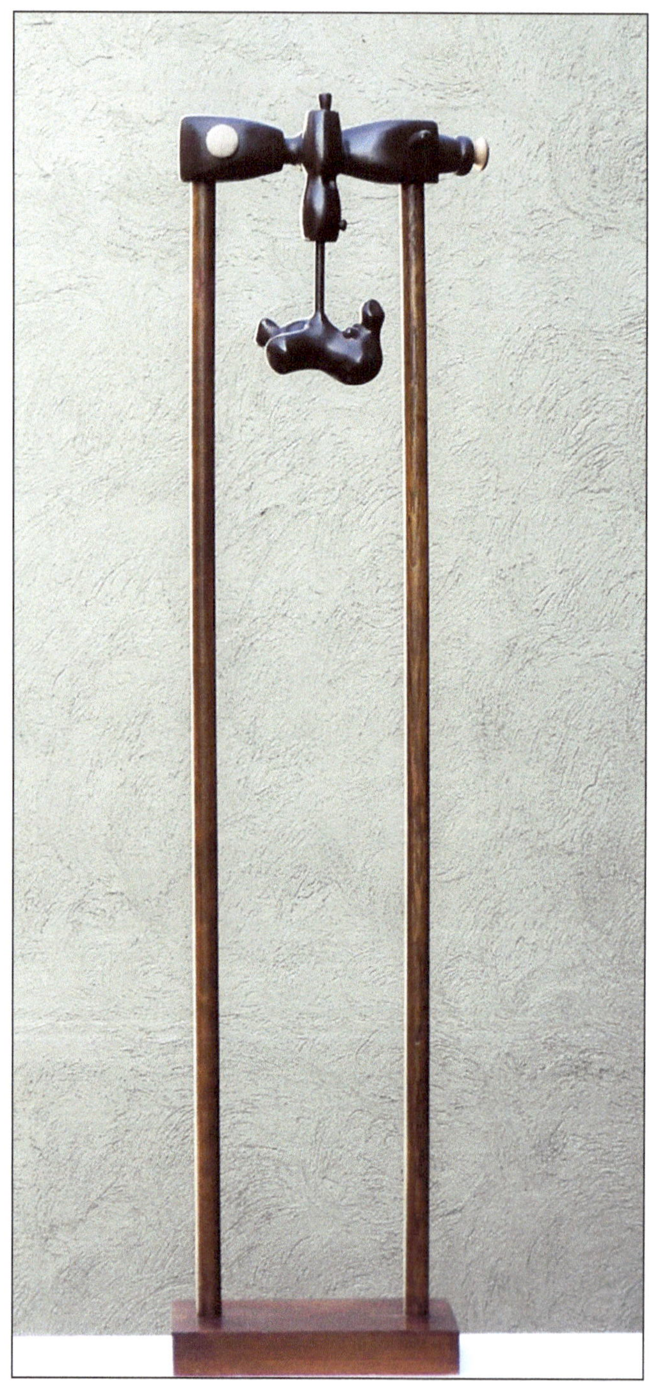

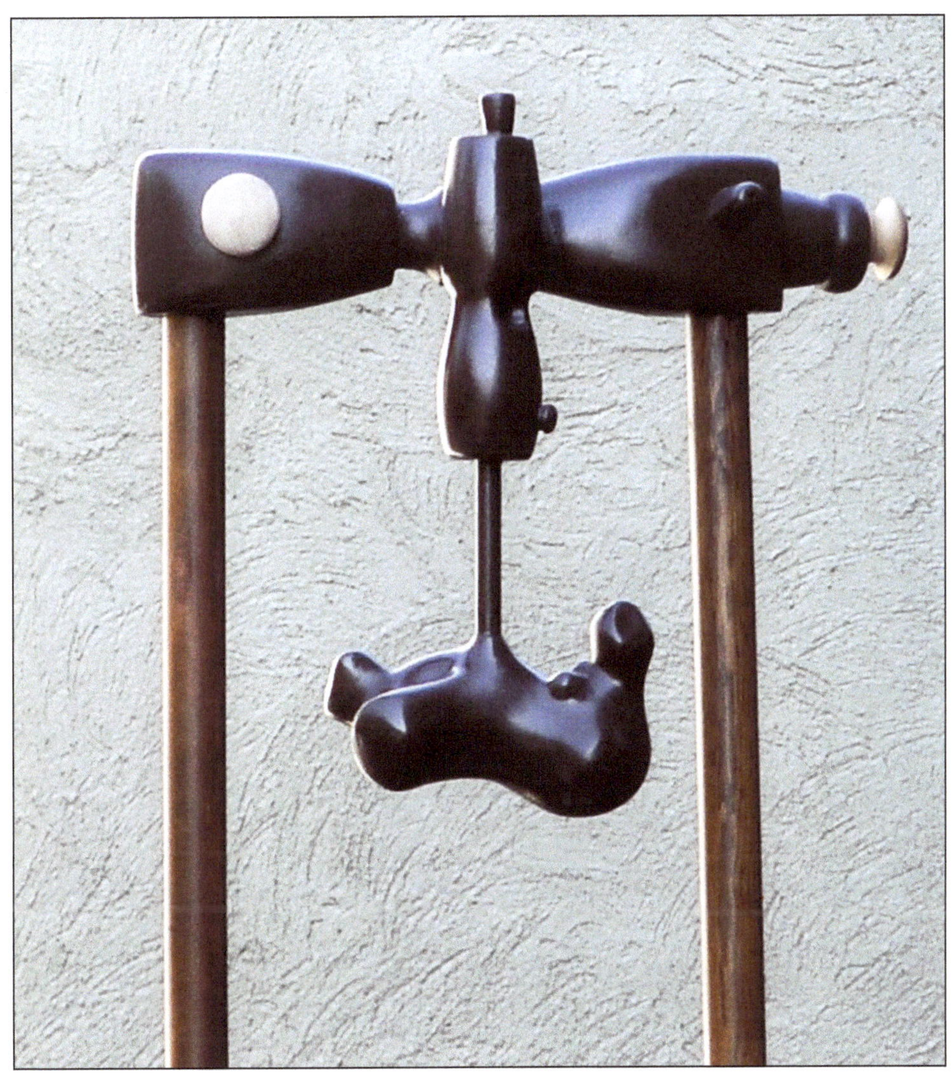

Dogon Mother and Child, 5 ft.7, constructed and carved wood with found objects, laminated clay (Bondo), and wooded dowels (at left, and close-up above).

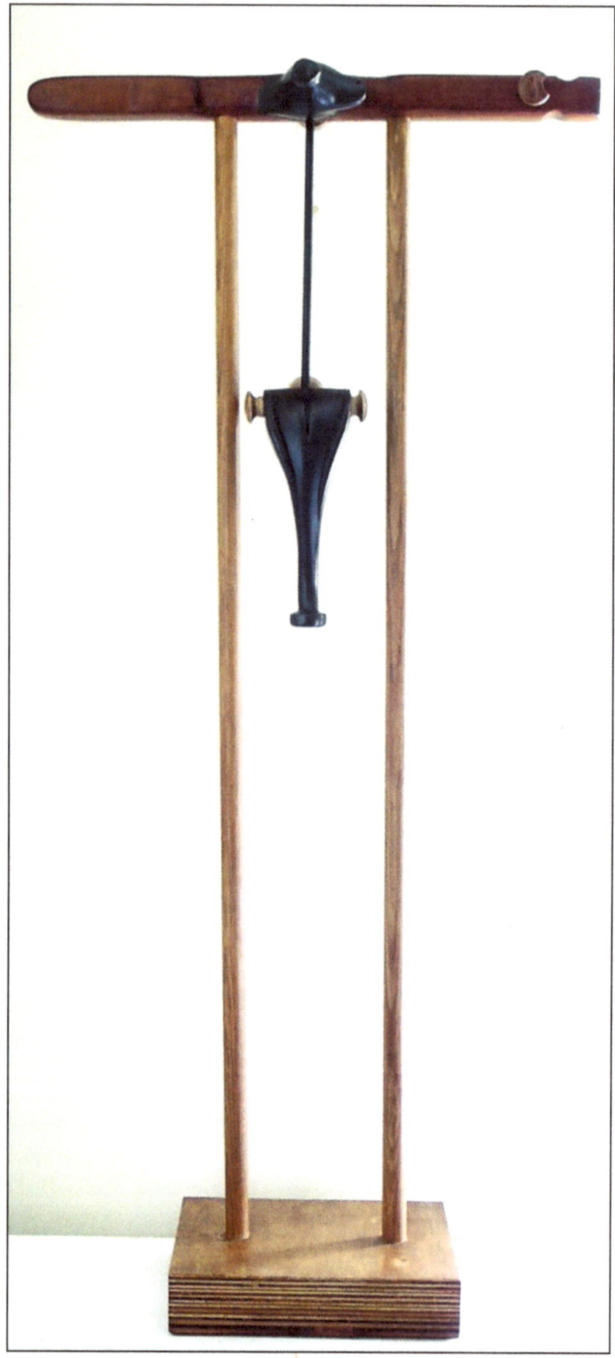

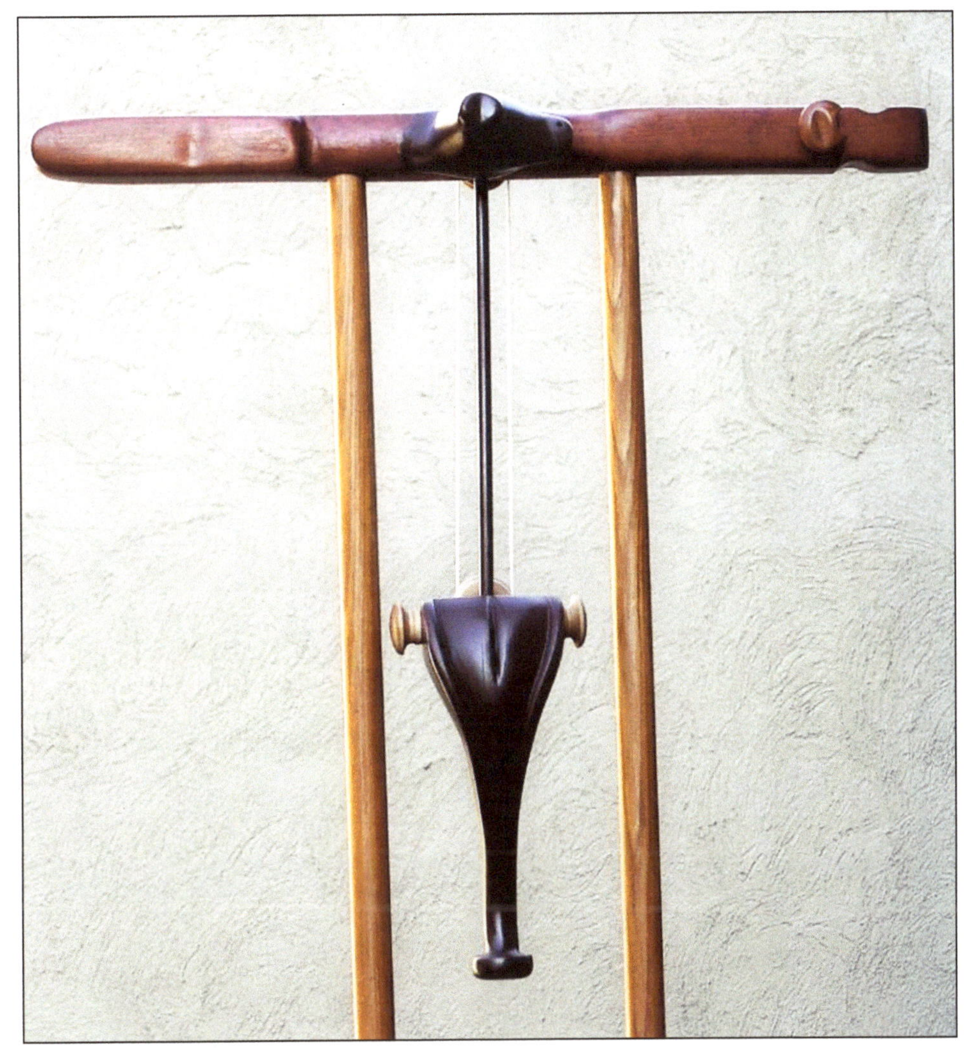

The Executioner's Song, 5ft. 8" carved and constructed wood, string, and found objects (at left, and close-up above).

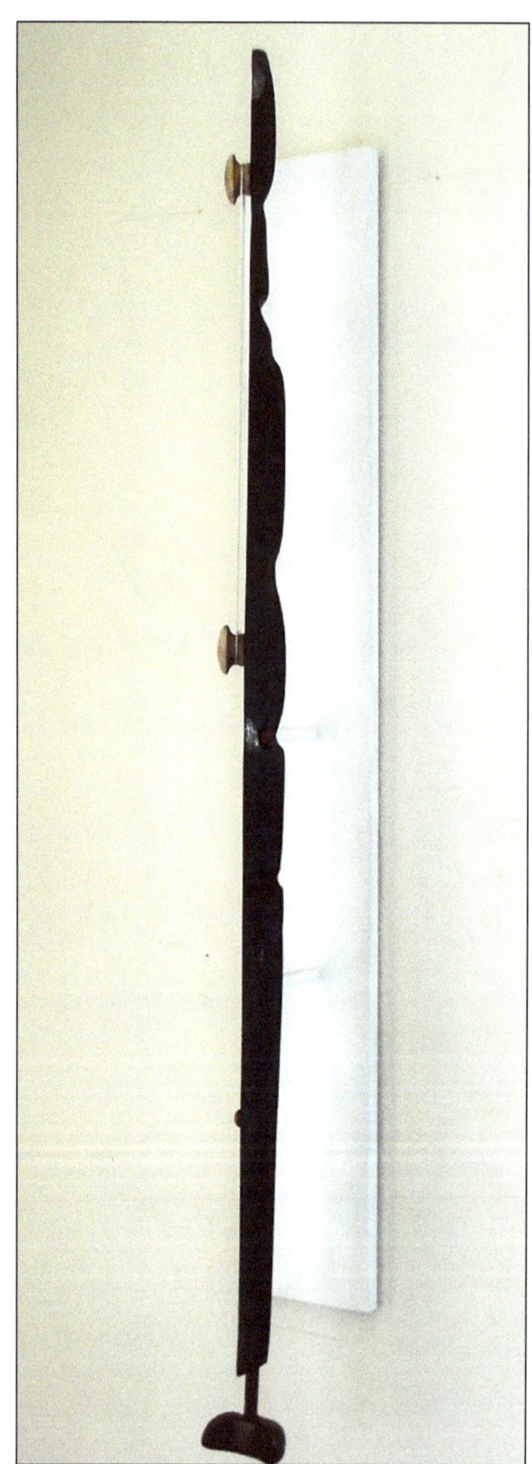

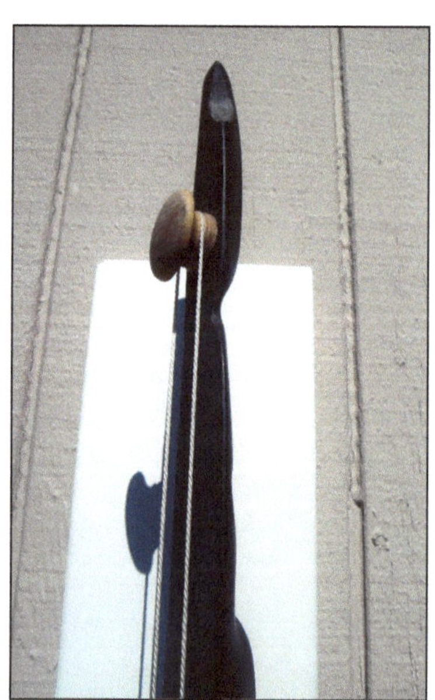

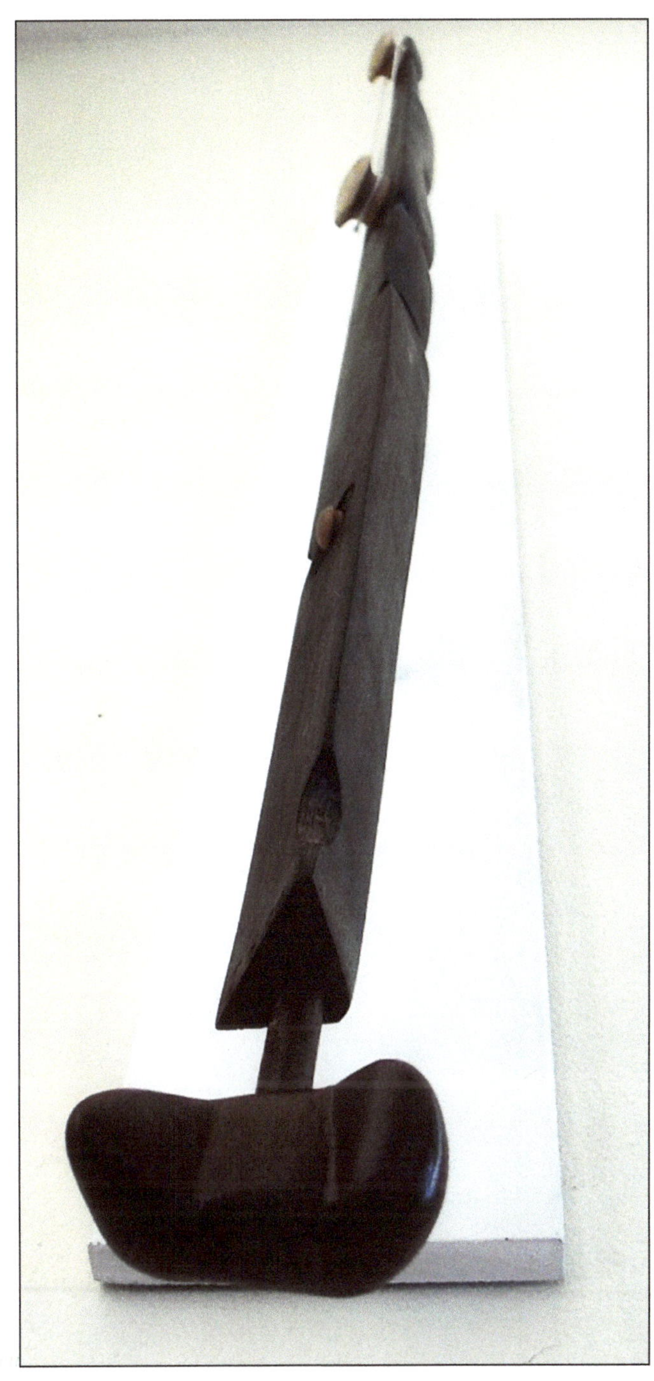

Out of Africa, 4 ft. long wall sculpture, carved ebony, string, fiber glass and found objects (at left, and above)

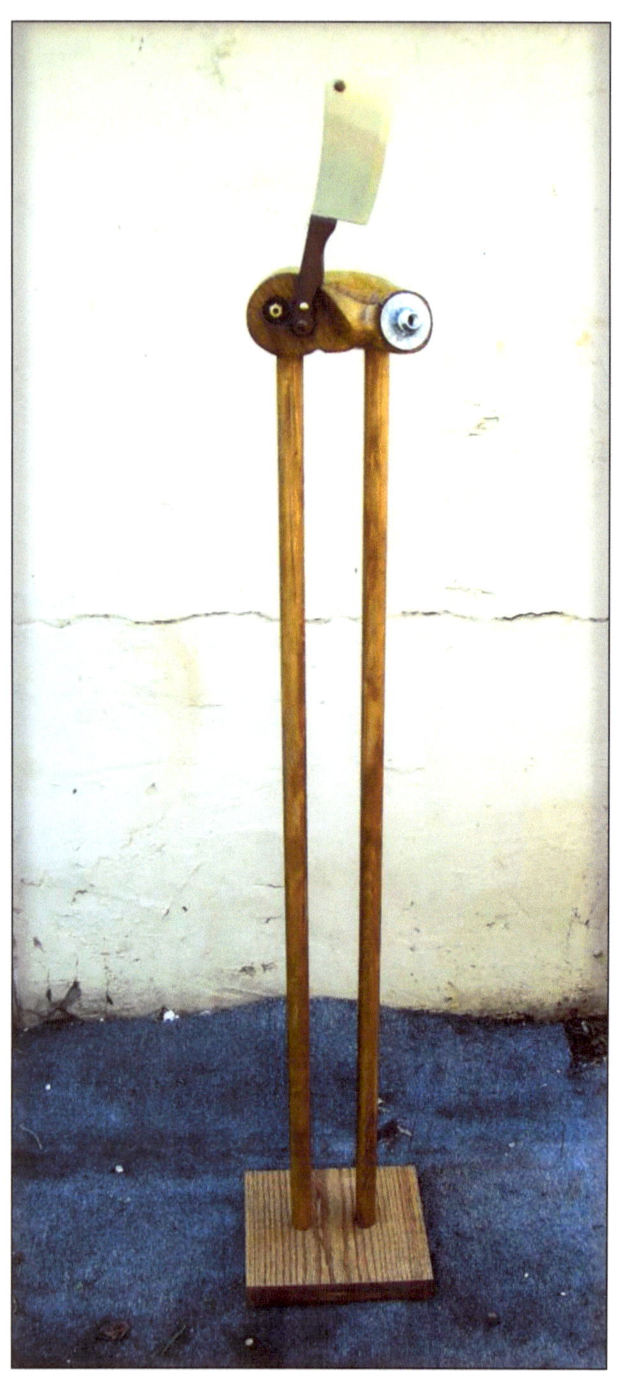

Rage Against the Machine, carved and constructed wood, found metal objects, and wood dowels, 5 ft. 5" tall (above, and at right)

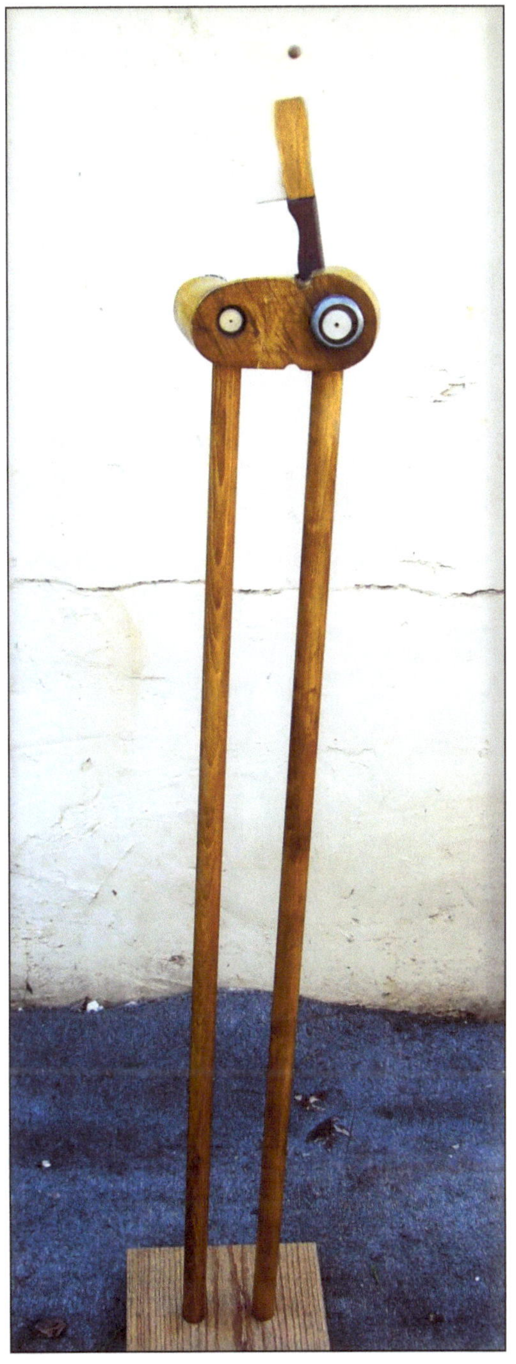

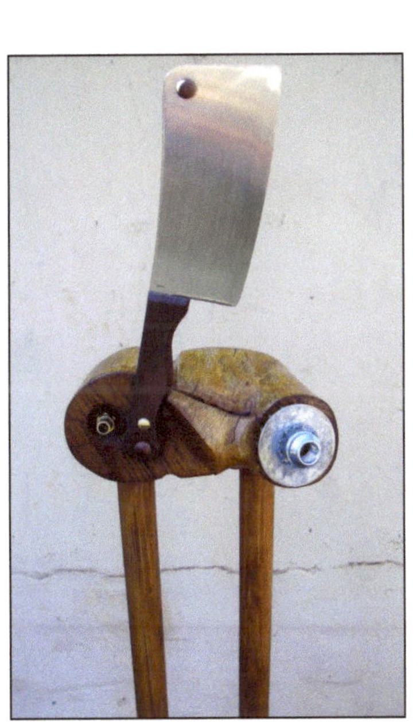

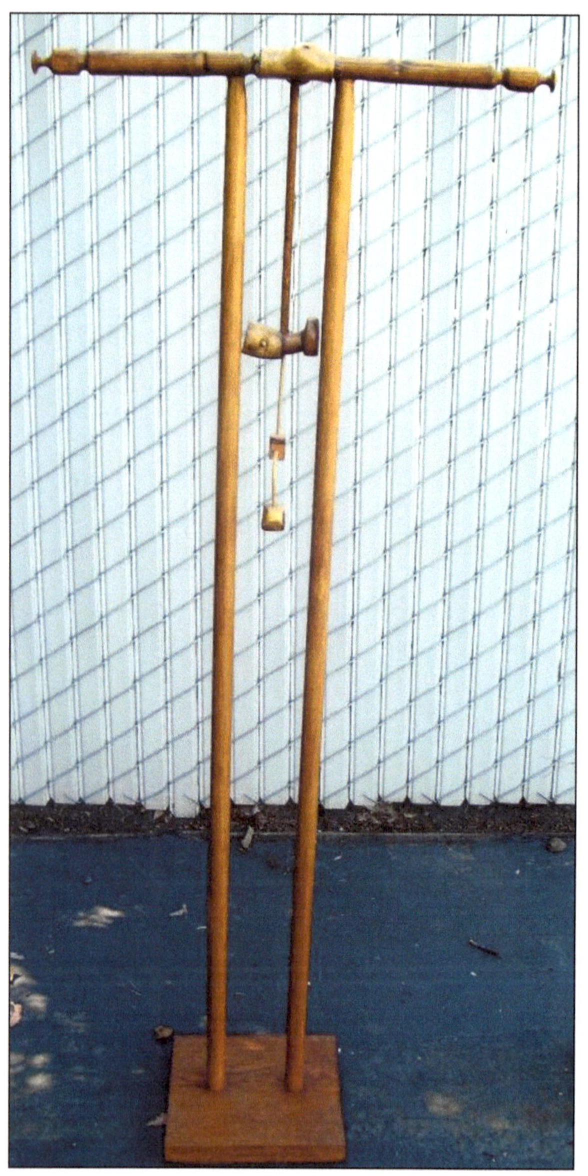

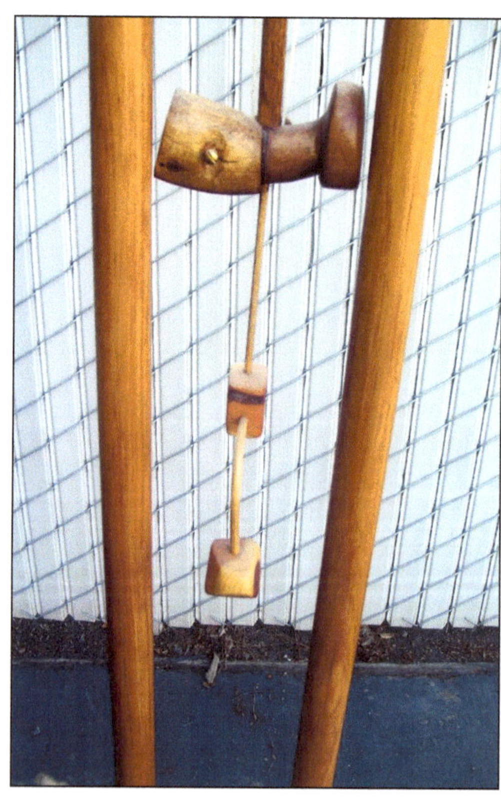

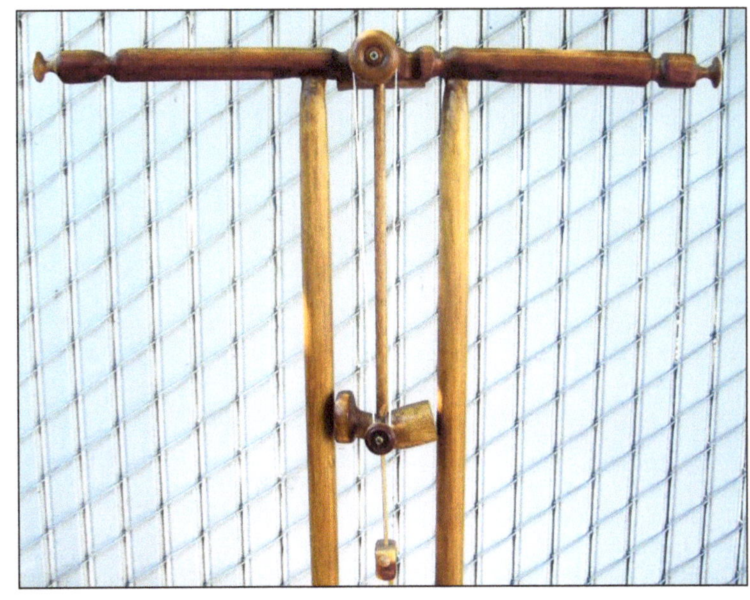

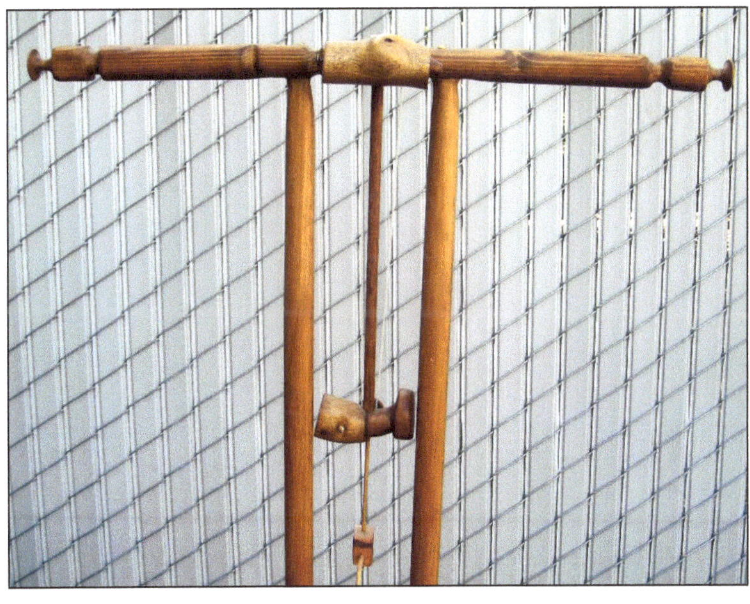

The Last Flight of Icarus, carved and constructed wood, string, found objects, and screws, 5 ft. 8 (at left, and close-ups above)

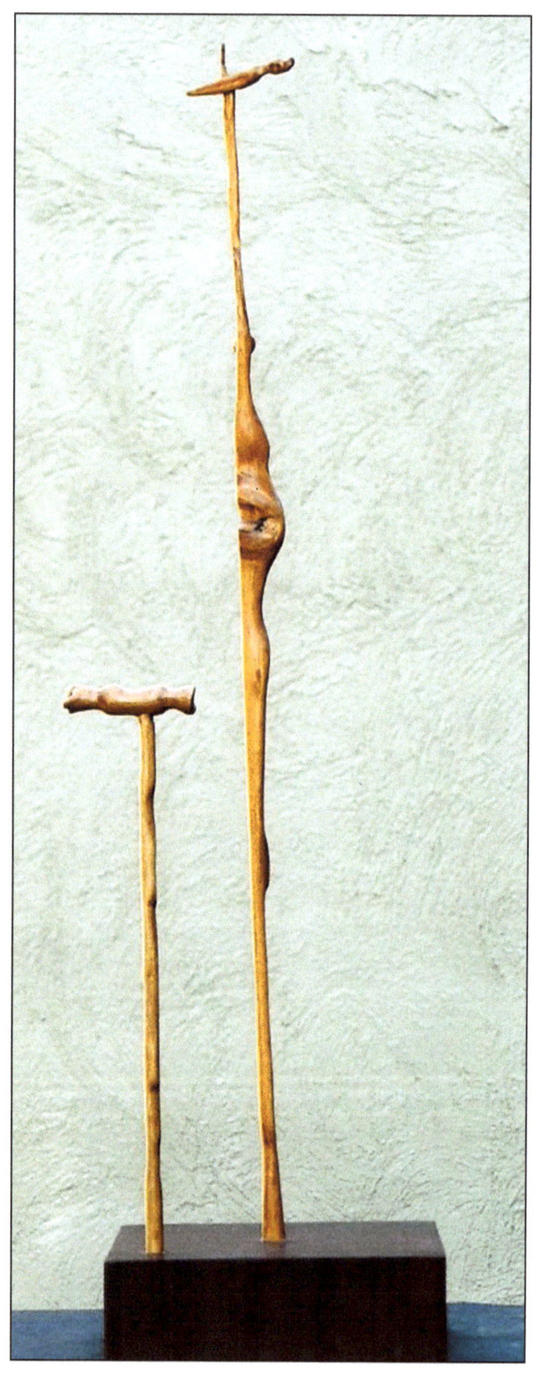

Strangers, carved and constructed wood, 32" long

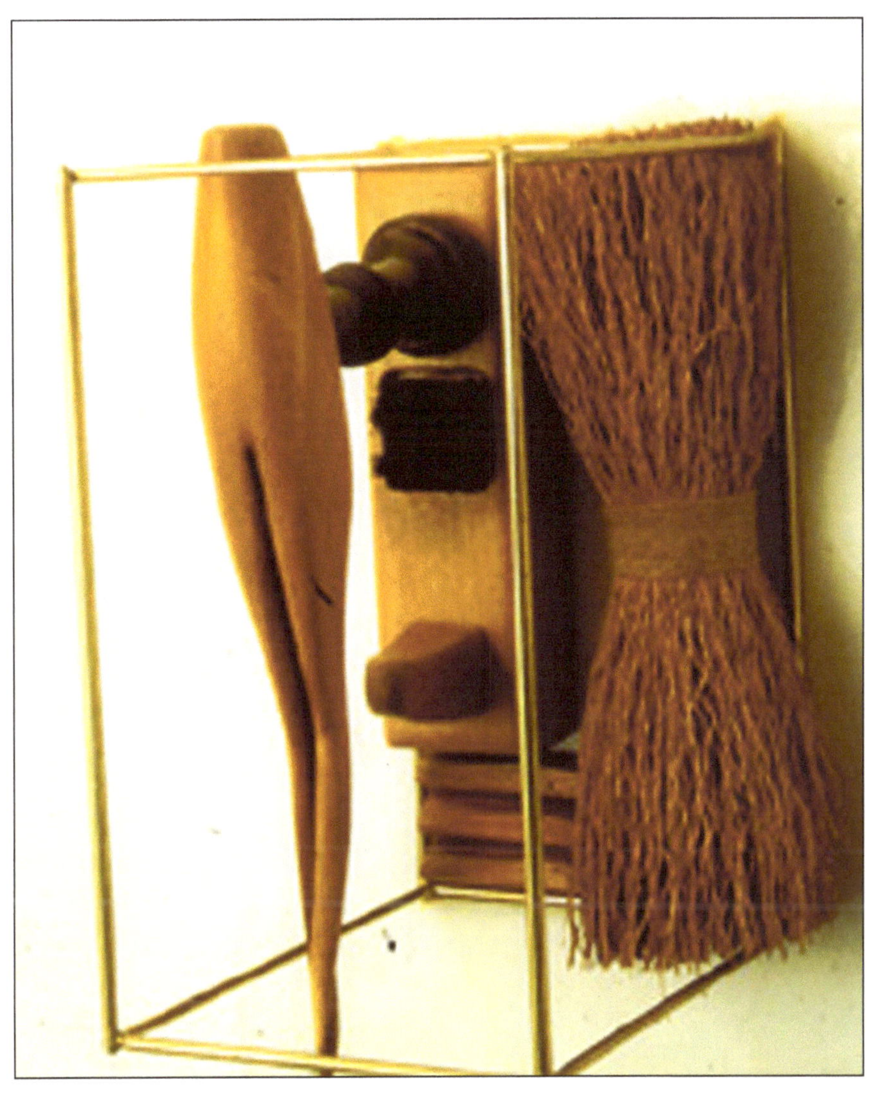

Roots, carved wood, Swedish found objects, and copper wire frame wall sculpture, 24" x 24"

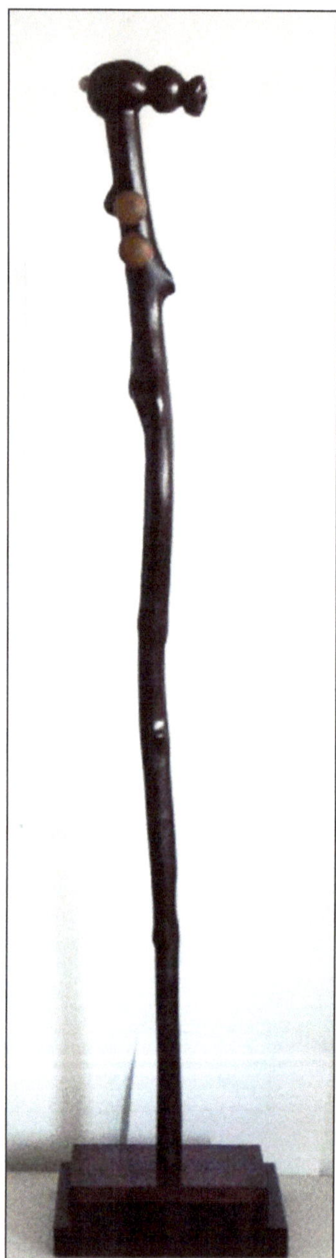

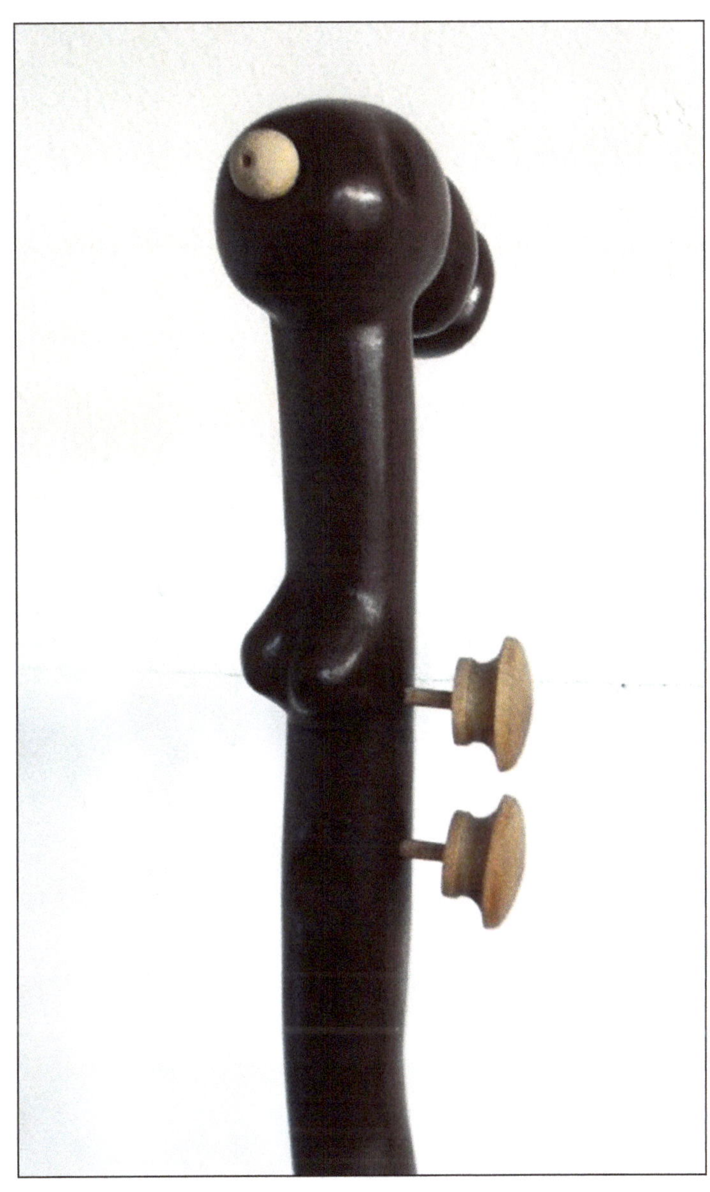

Homage to Billie Holiday, clay (bondo), wood, and found objects, 5 ft. 6" (at left, and close-up at right)

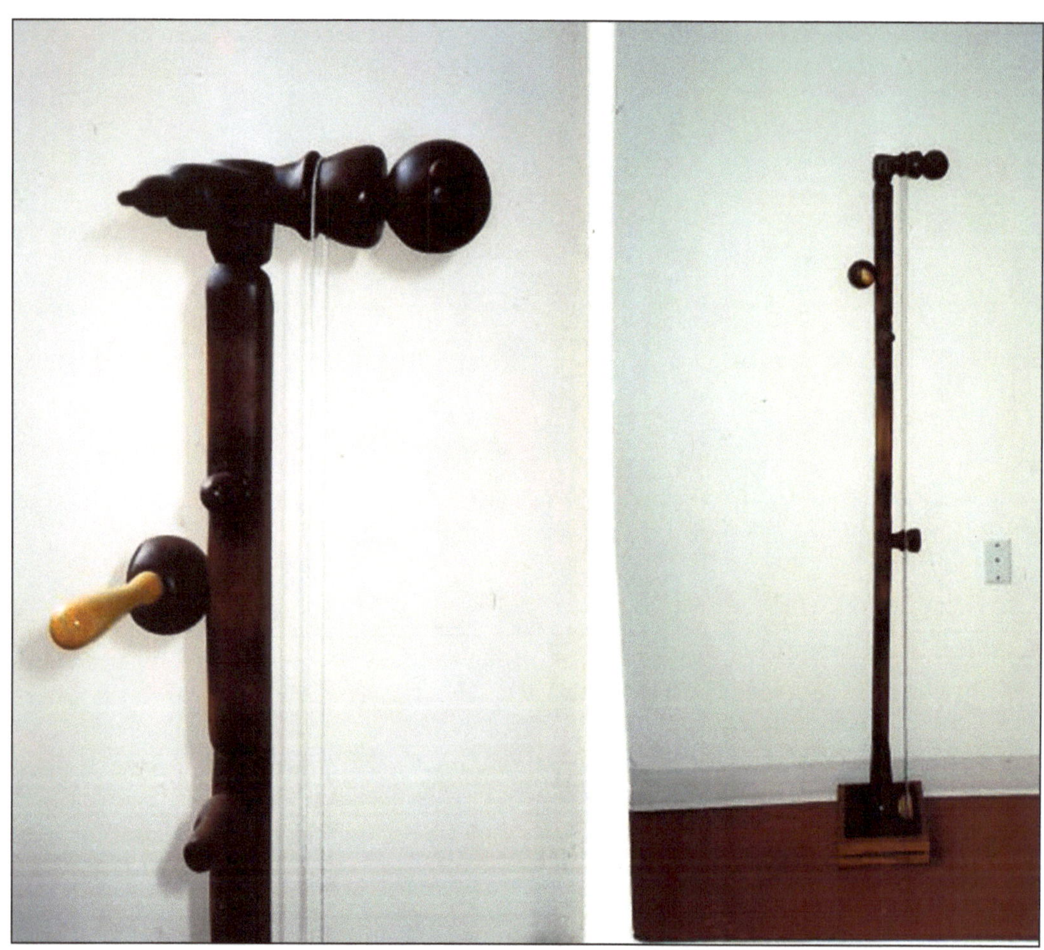

Yo Yo Your Mama, carved wood, found objects, string, 5 ft. long

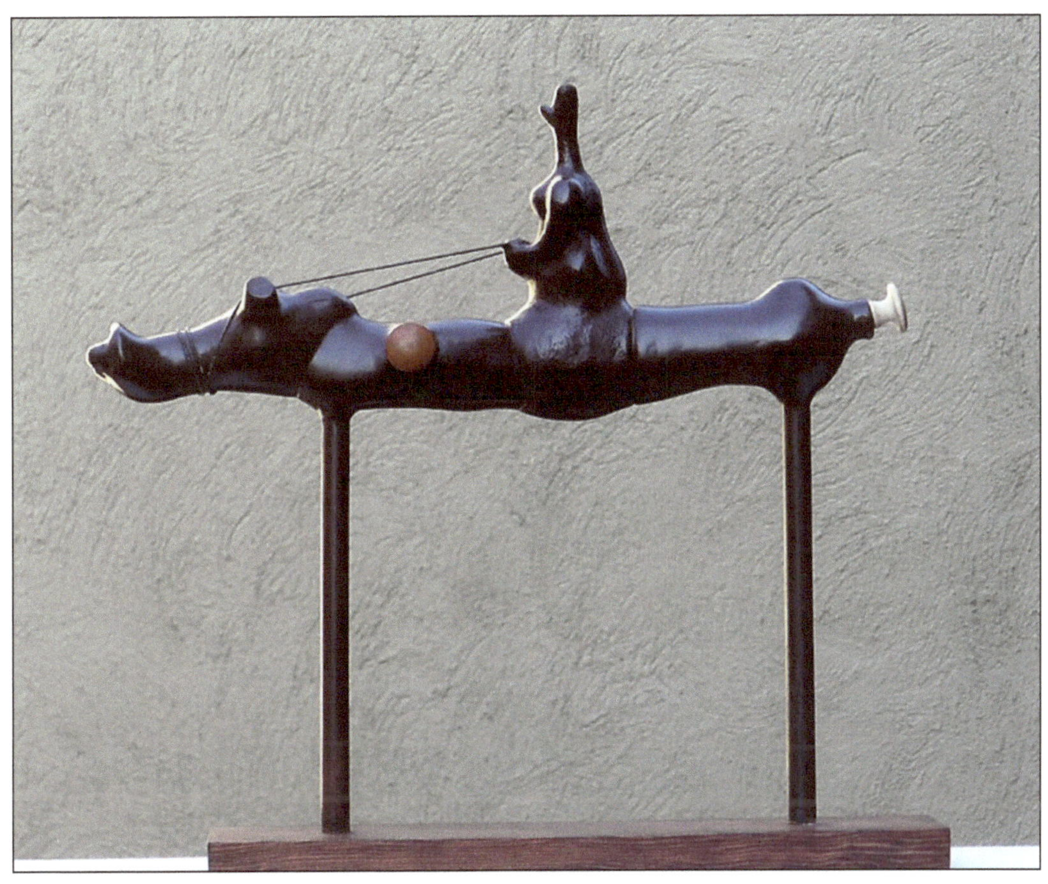

Night Rider, laminated clay (bondo), leather, wood, and found objects. 8" high, 26" long

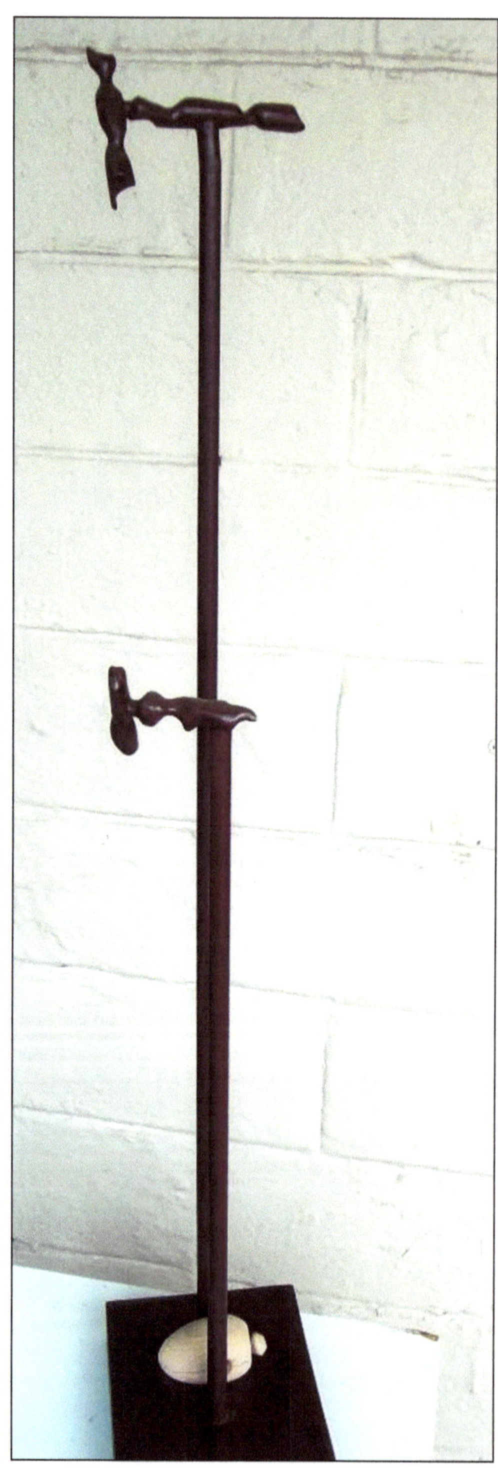

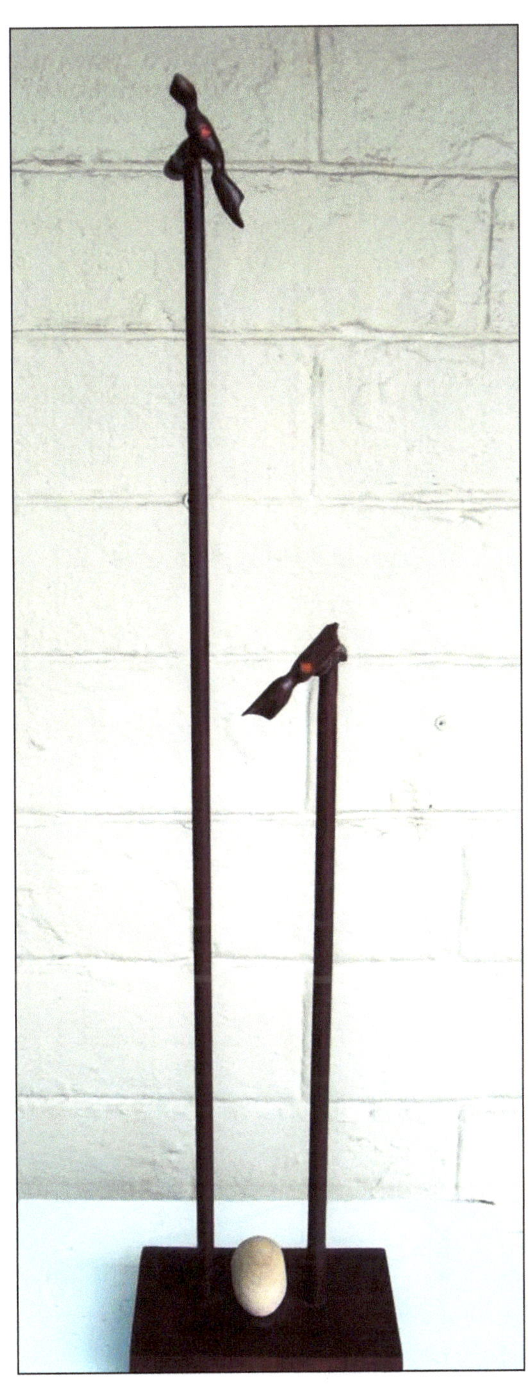

The Birth of Tragedy, carved and painted wood, 28" high (at left, and above)

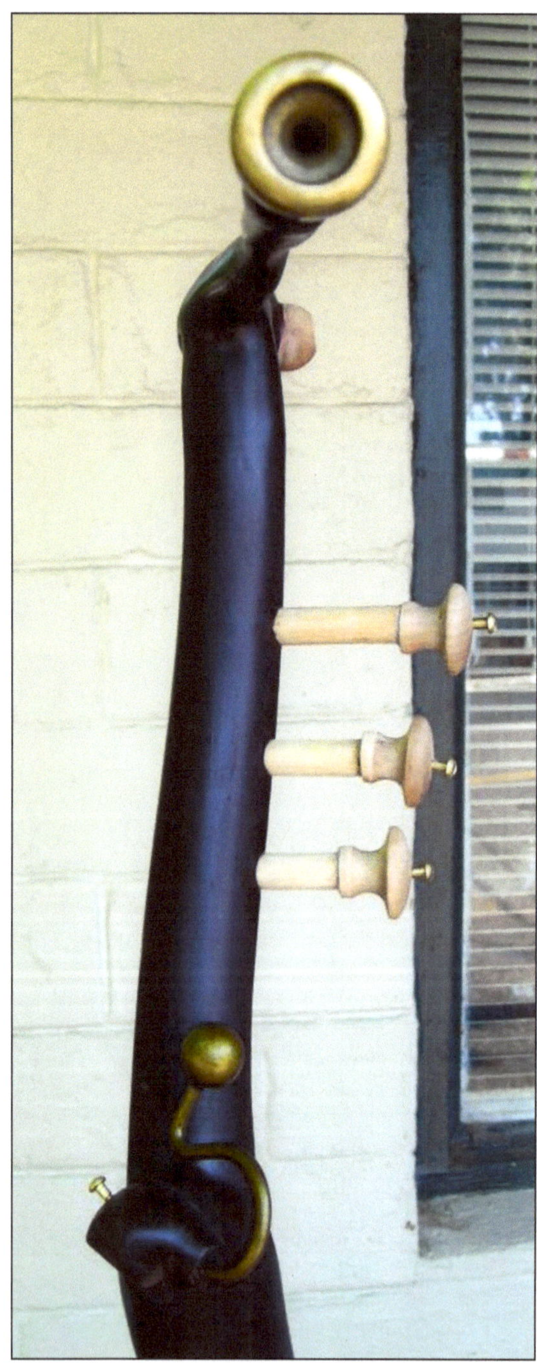

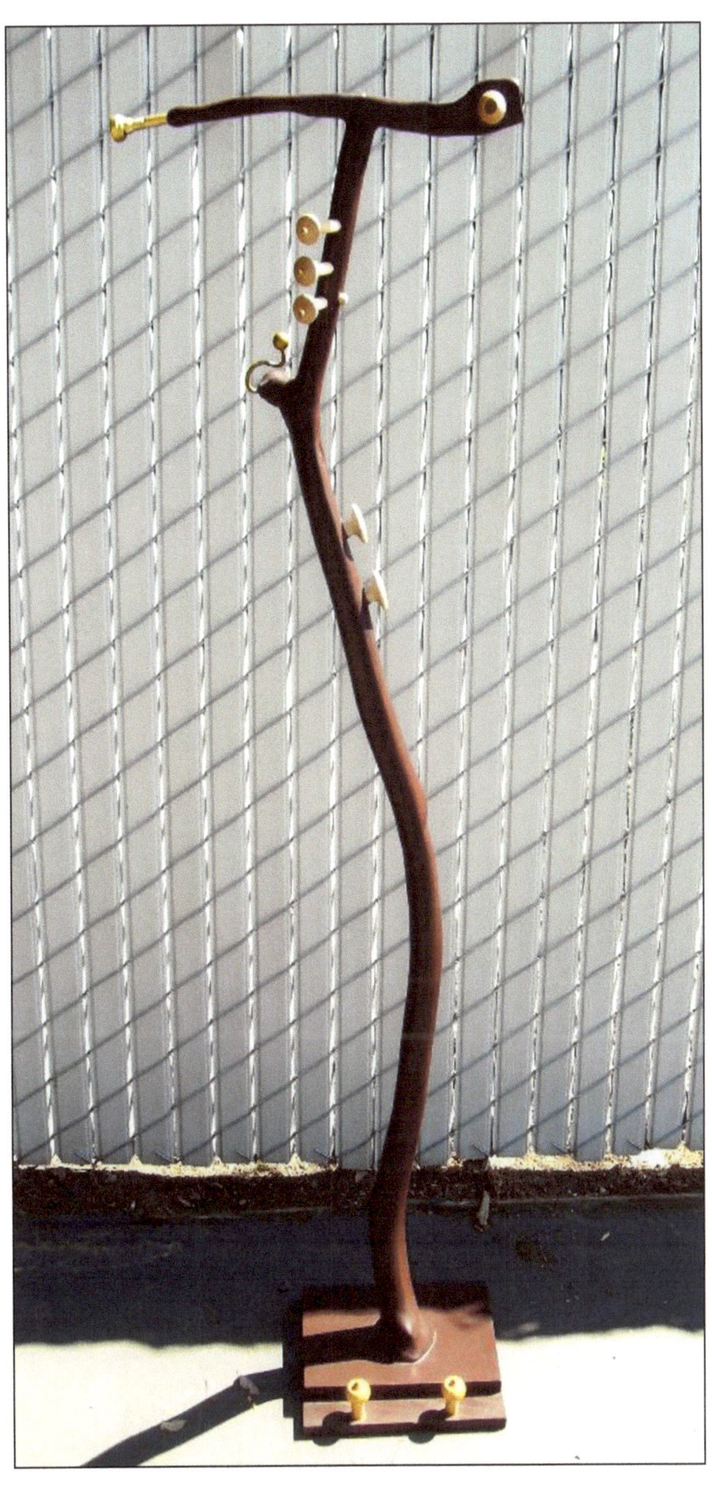

Miles Davis Diggin' Charlie "Bird " Parker. 5 ft. 8" laminated wood, found objects, and trumpet mouth piece (at left, and above)

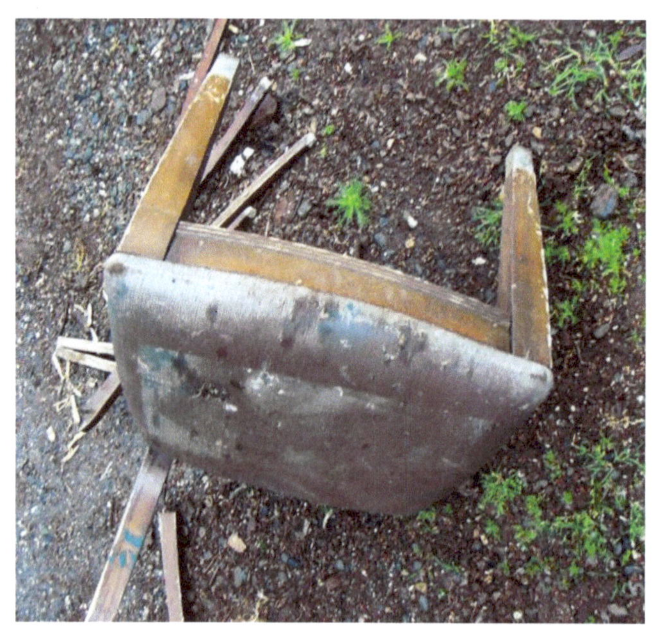

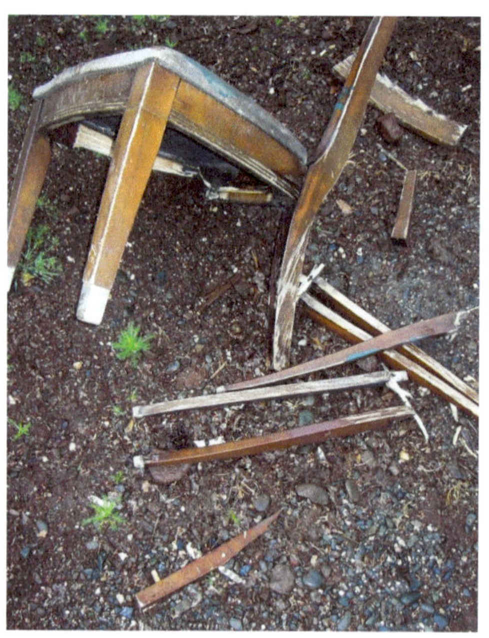

Drive-By Street Thug - A Predator, carved wood, found objects, and copper screws, 31" x 2" x 14", movable middle parts (above, at right)

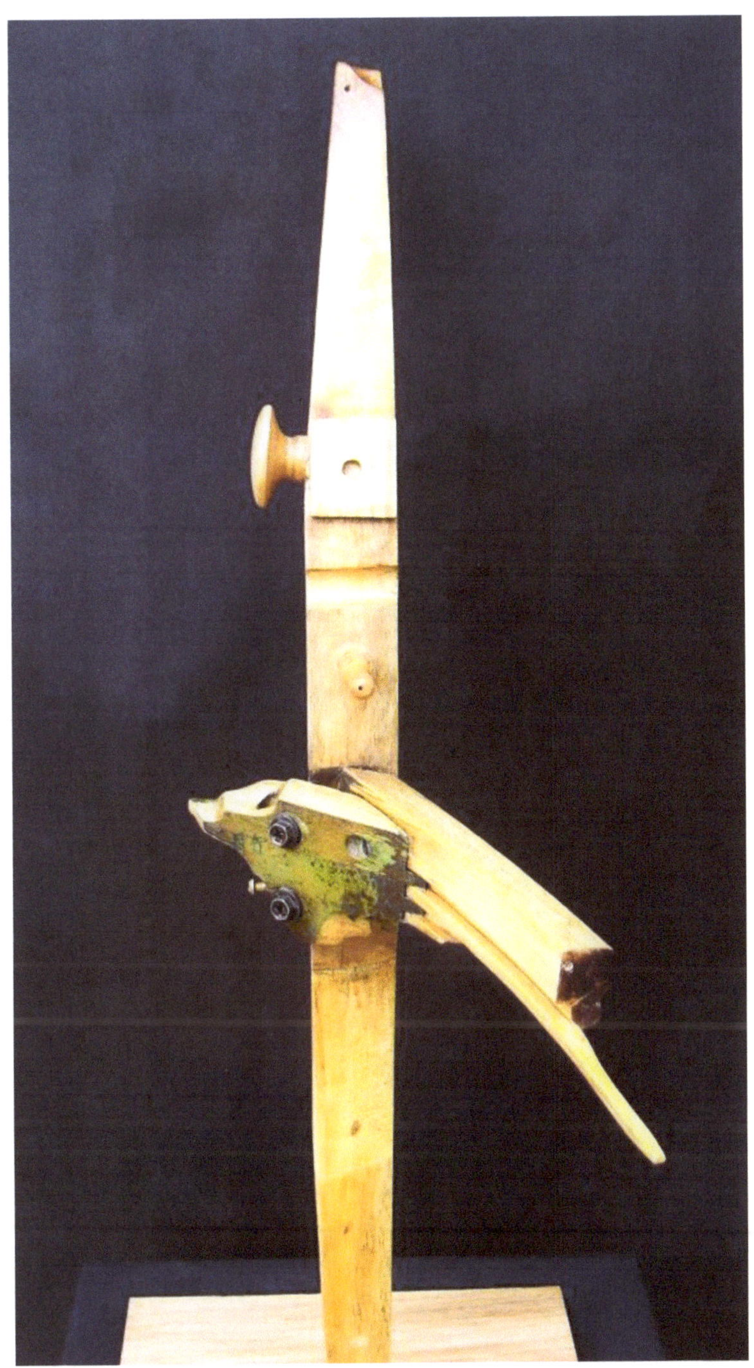

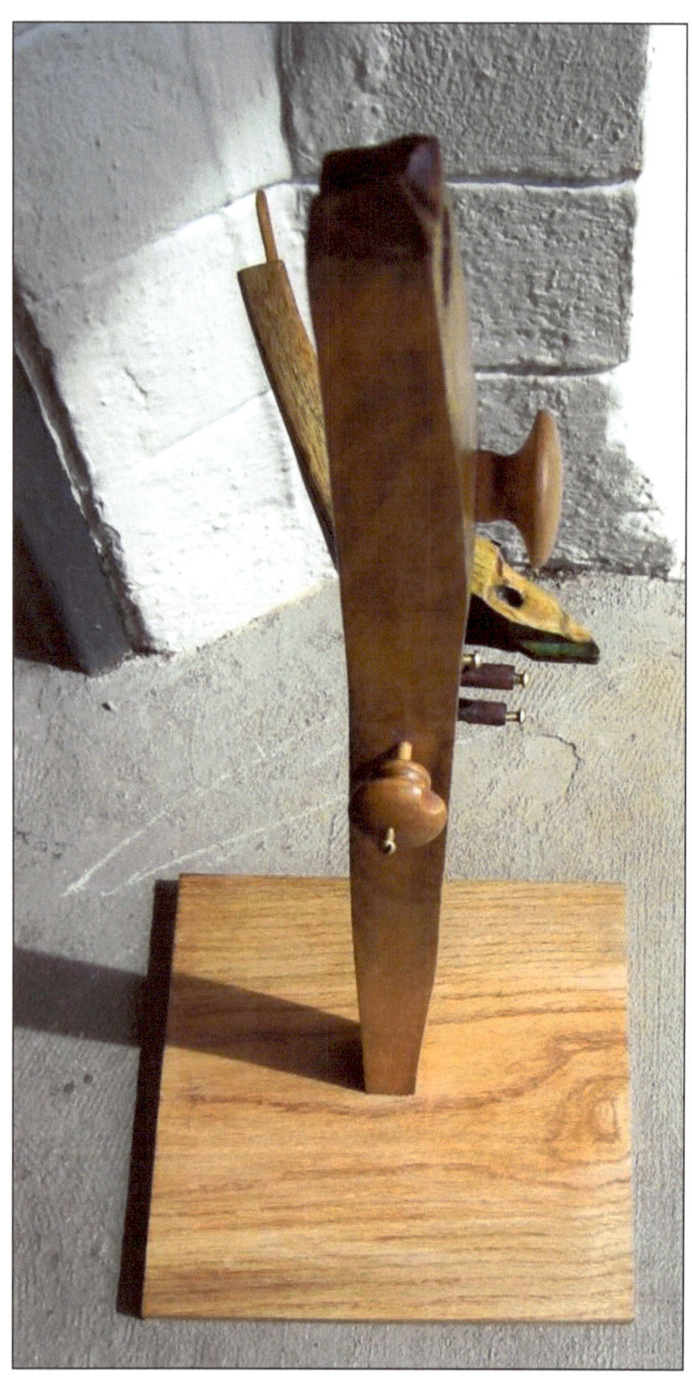

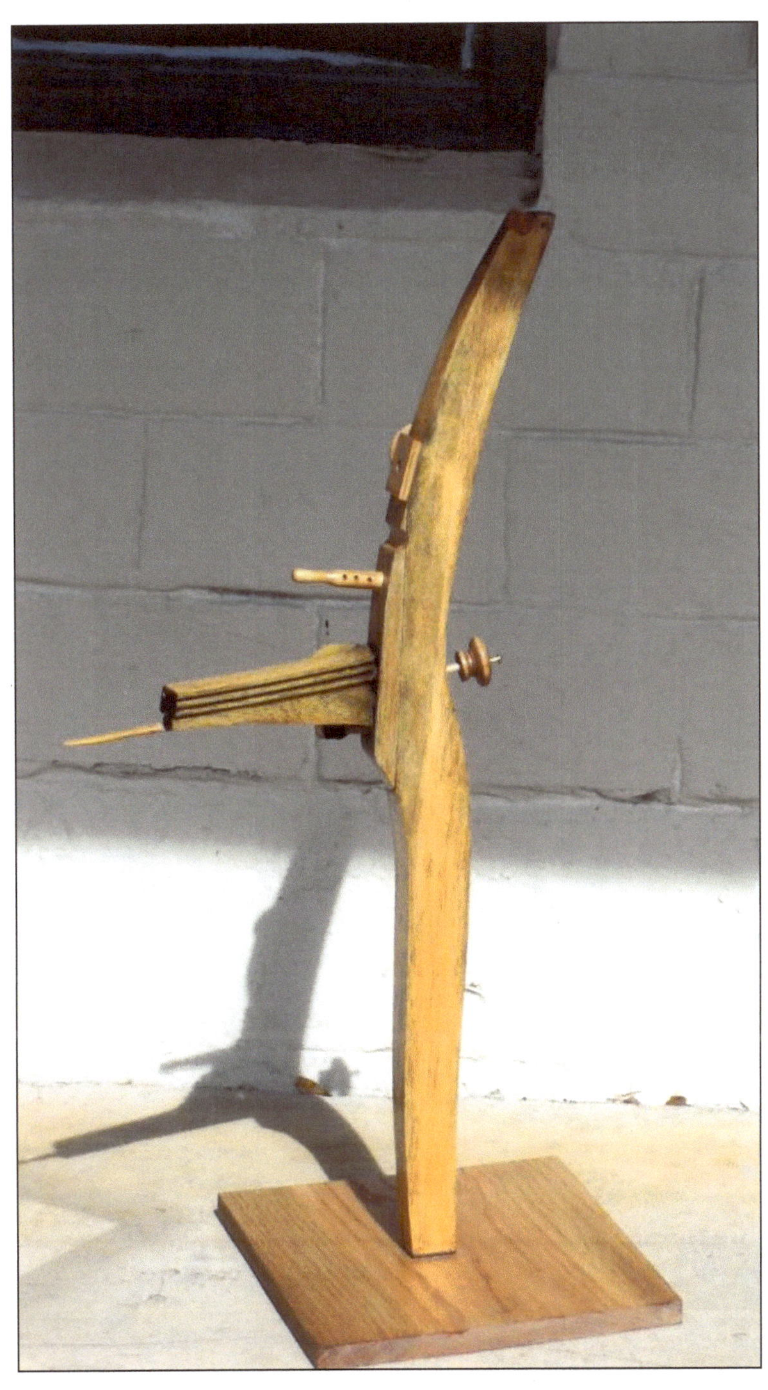

Drive-By Street Thug - A Predator, carved wood, found objects, and copper screws, 31" x 2" x 14", movable middle parts (at left, above)

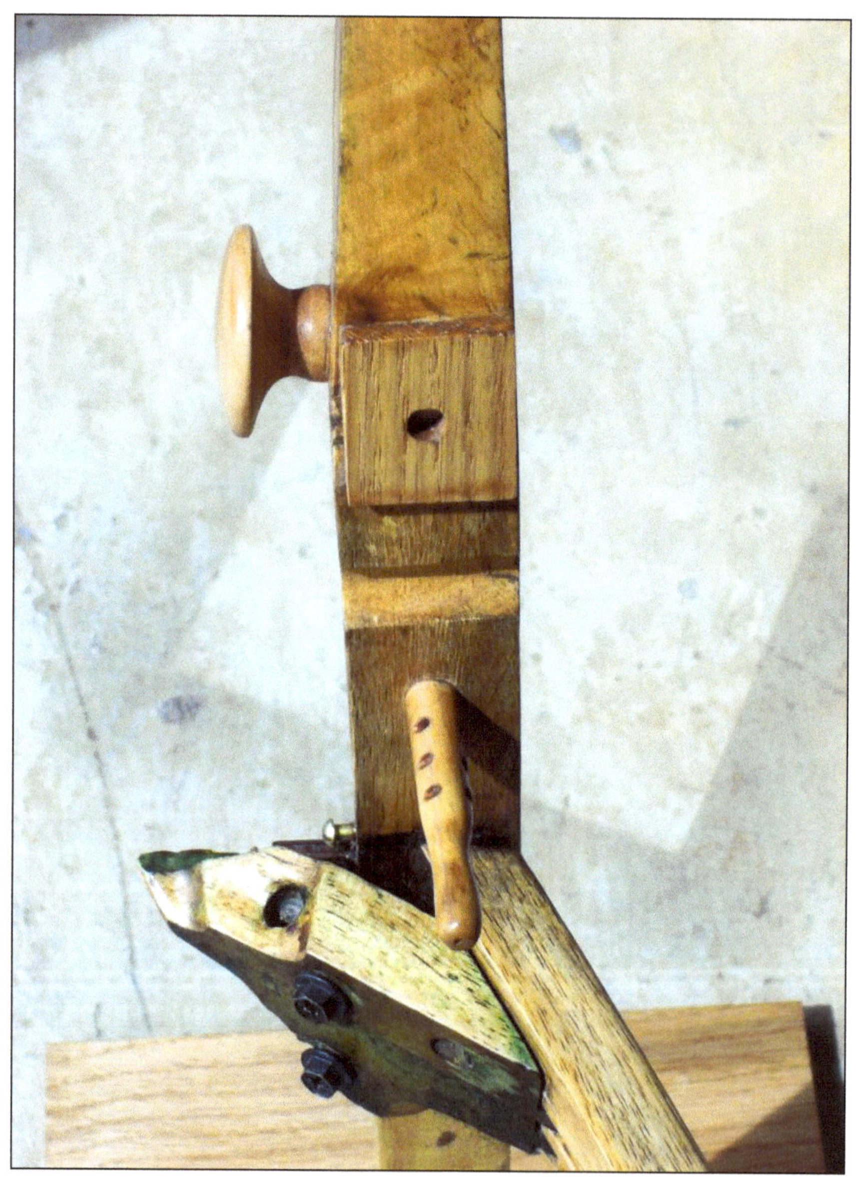

Drive-By Street Thug A Predator, carved wood, found objects, and copper screws, 31" x 2" x 14", movable middle parts (close-up above)

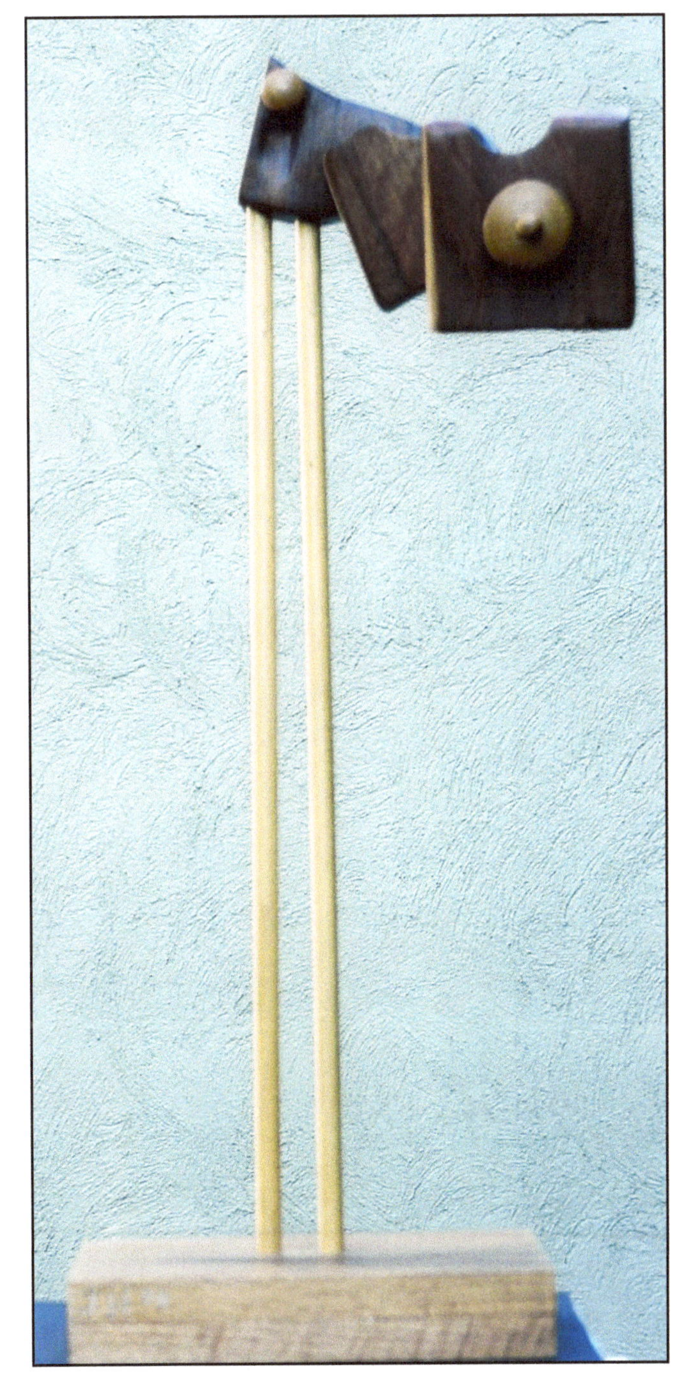

Tic Tac Toe, carved wood and found objects, 24" x 9"

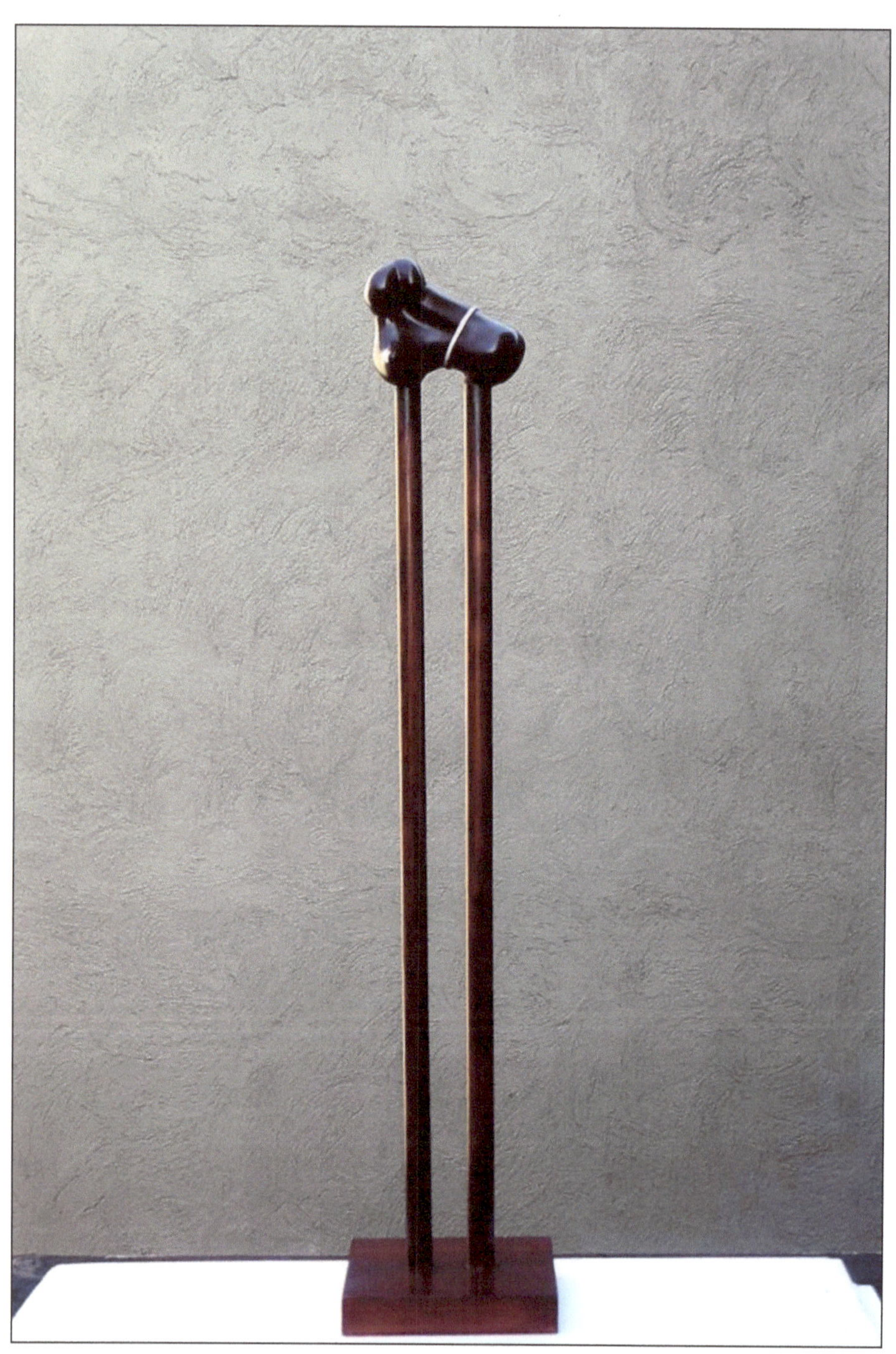

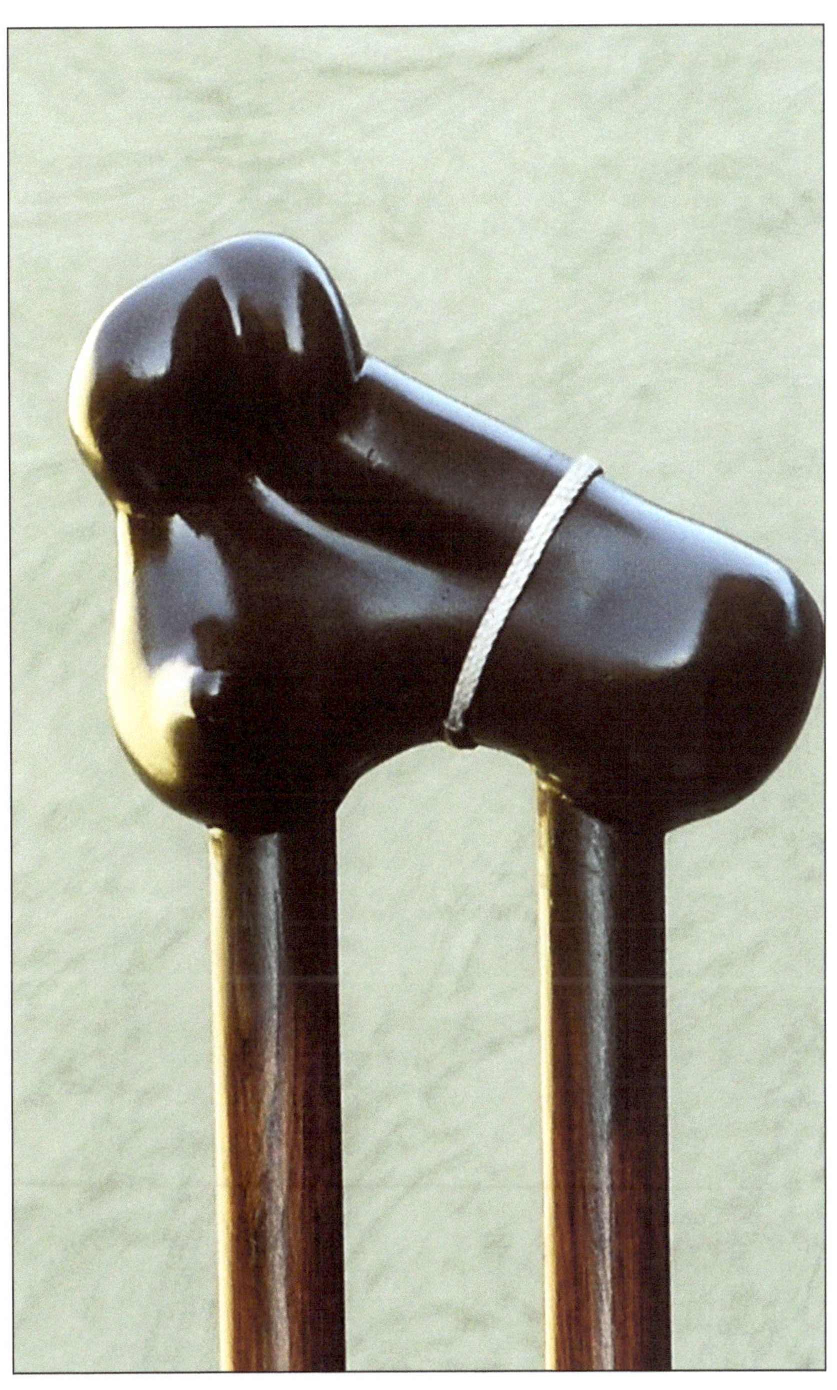

Captured Forms in Space, laminated clay (bondo) and string,
4 ft. tall (at left, and close-up above)

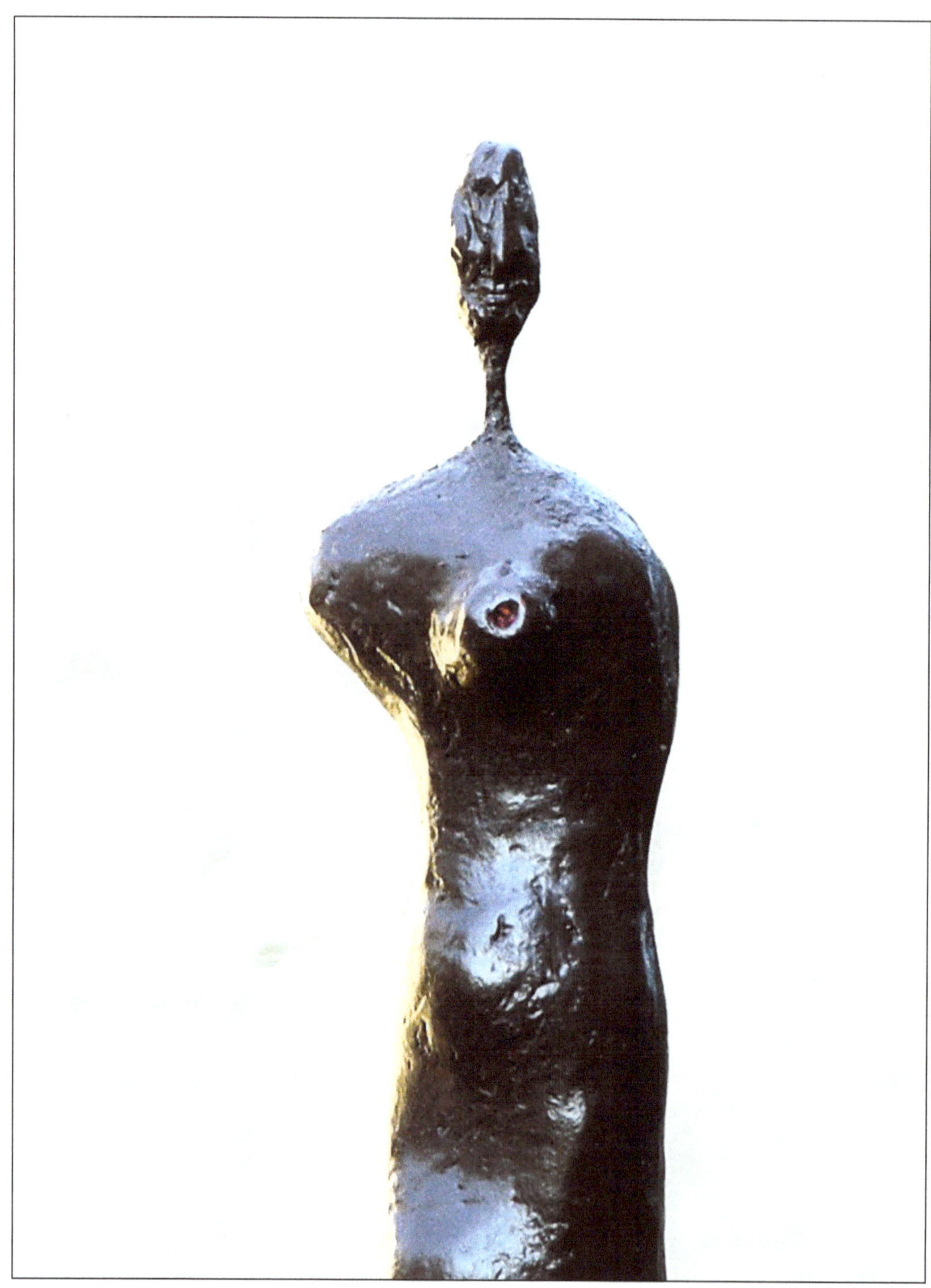

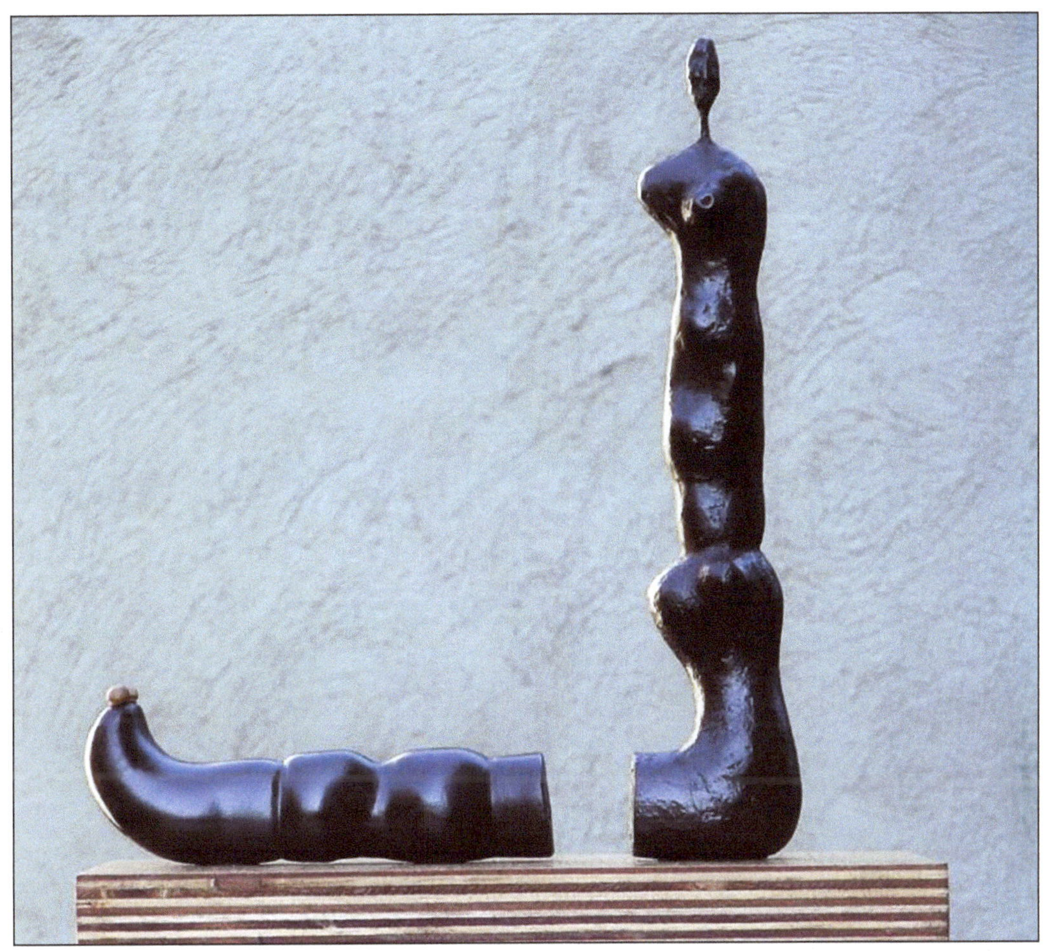

Anthony and Cleopatra Divided, laminated clay, 14 x 12" (at left, and above)

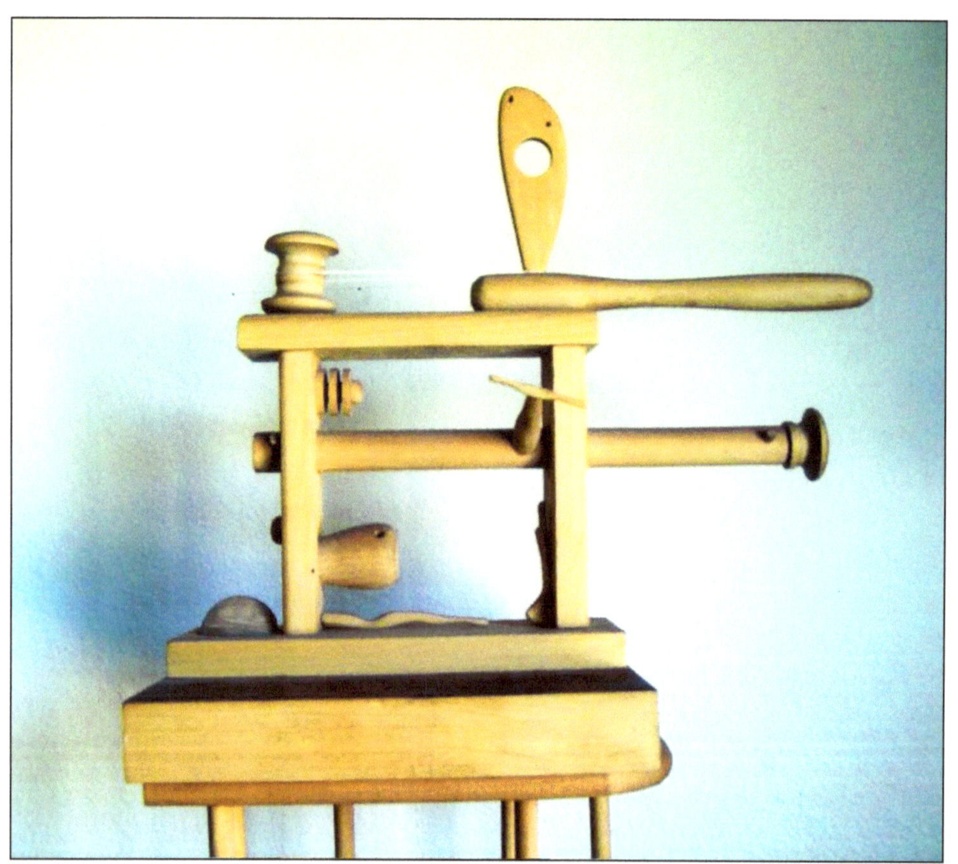

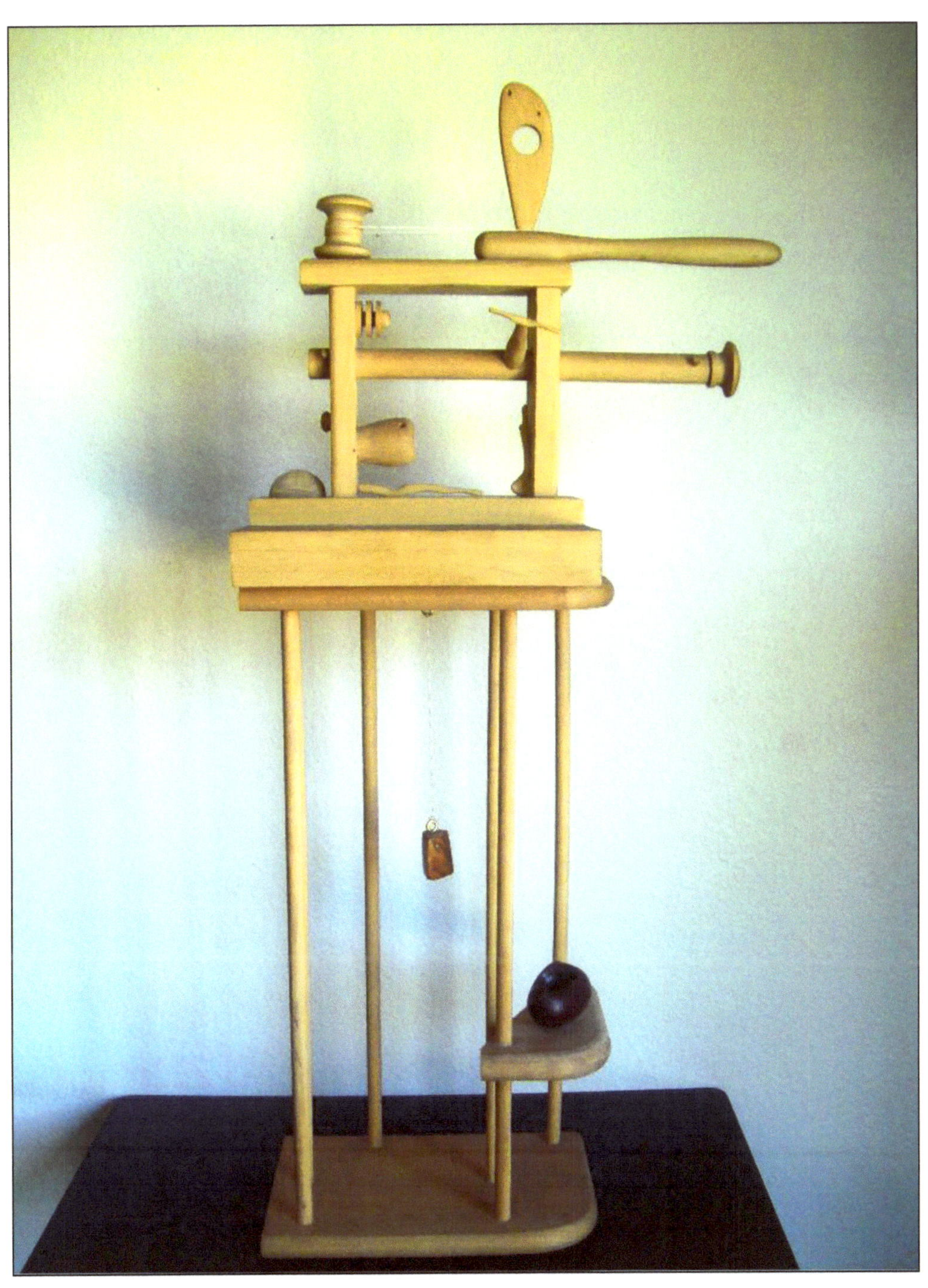

The Nightmare at 4.a.m., Homage to Giacometti's Palace at 4 a.m. (at left, and above)

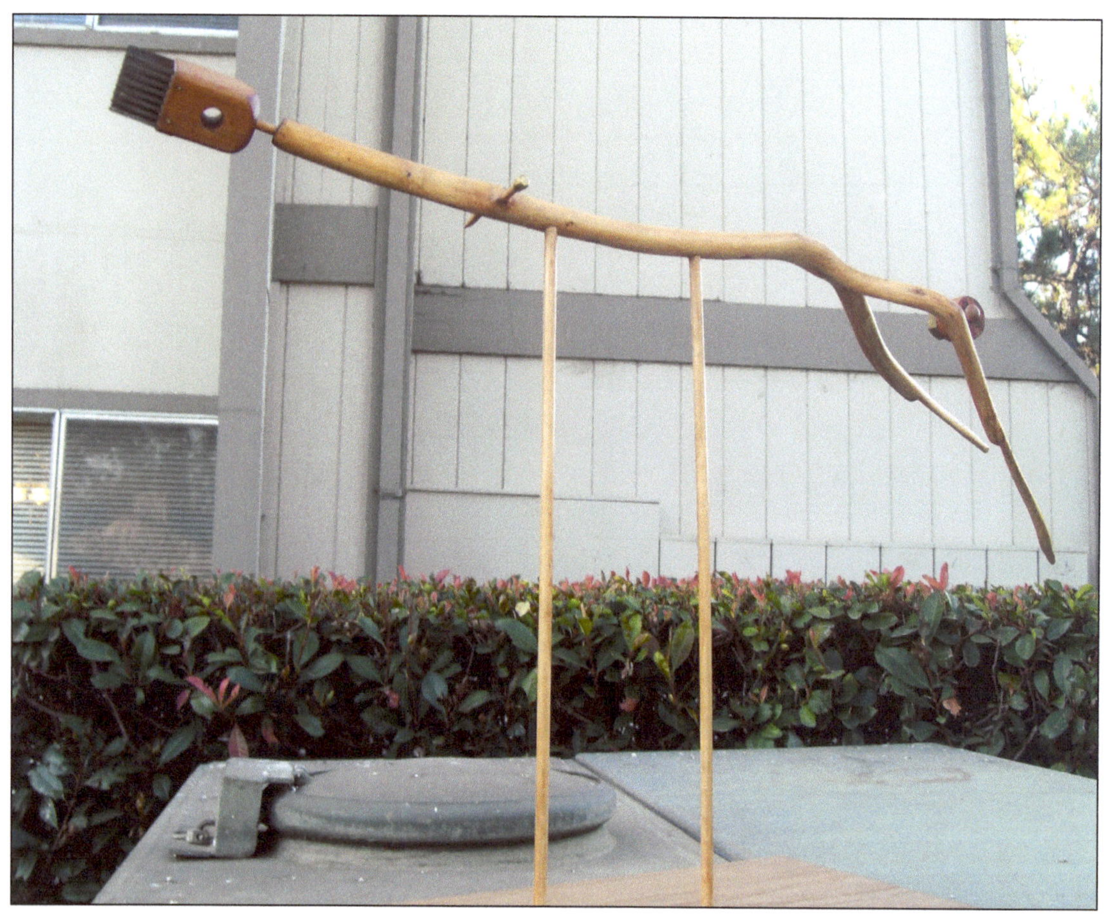

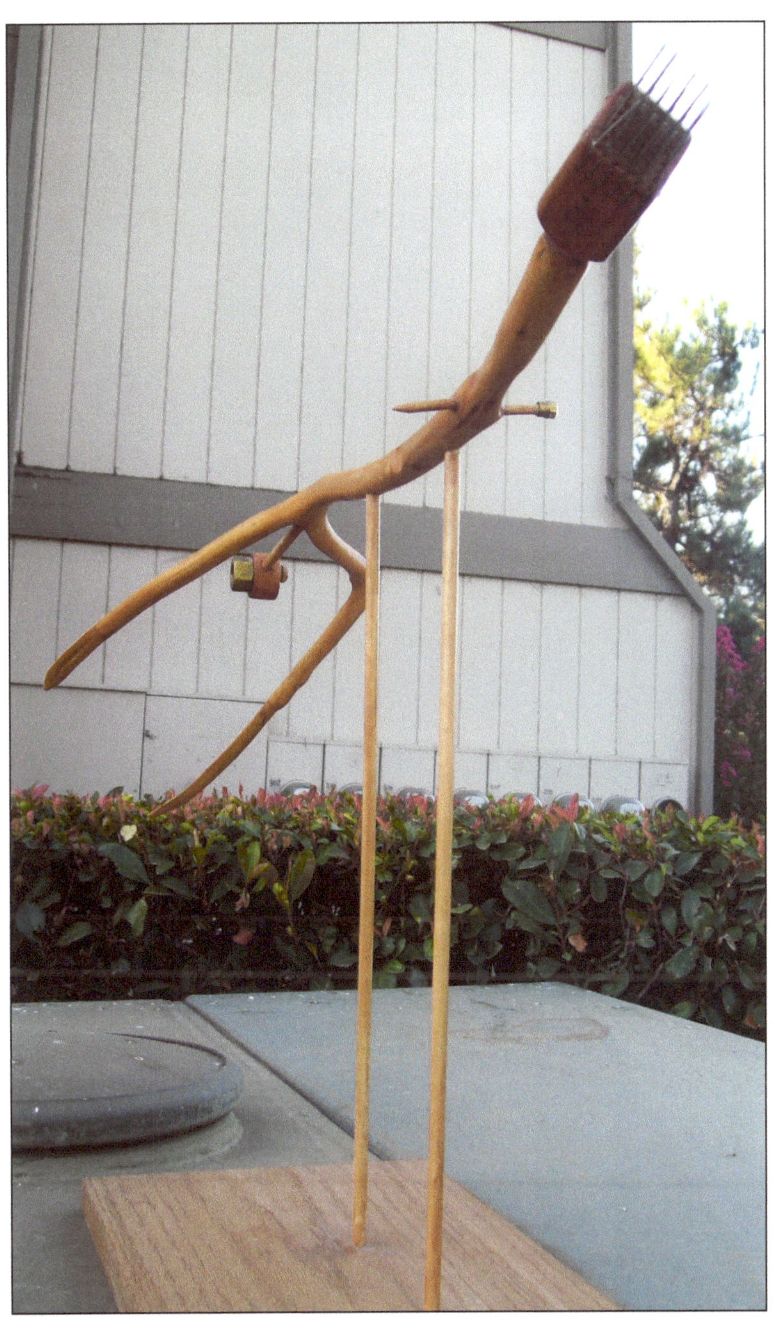

The Drugged Kid, mixed media, carved wood and found objects, 27" long (at left, and above)

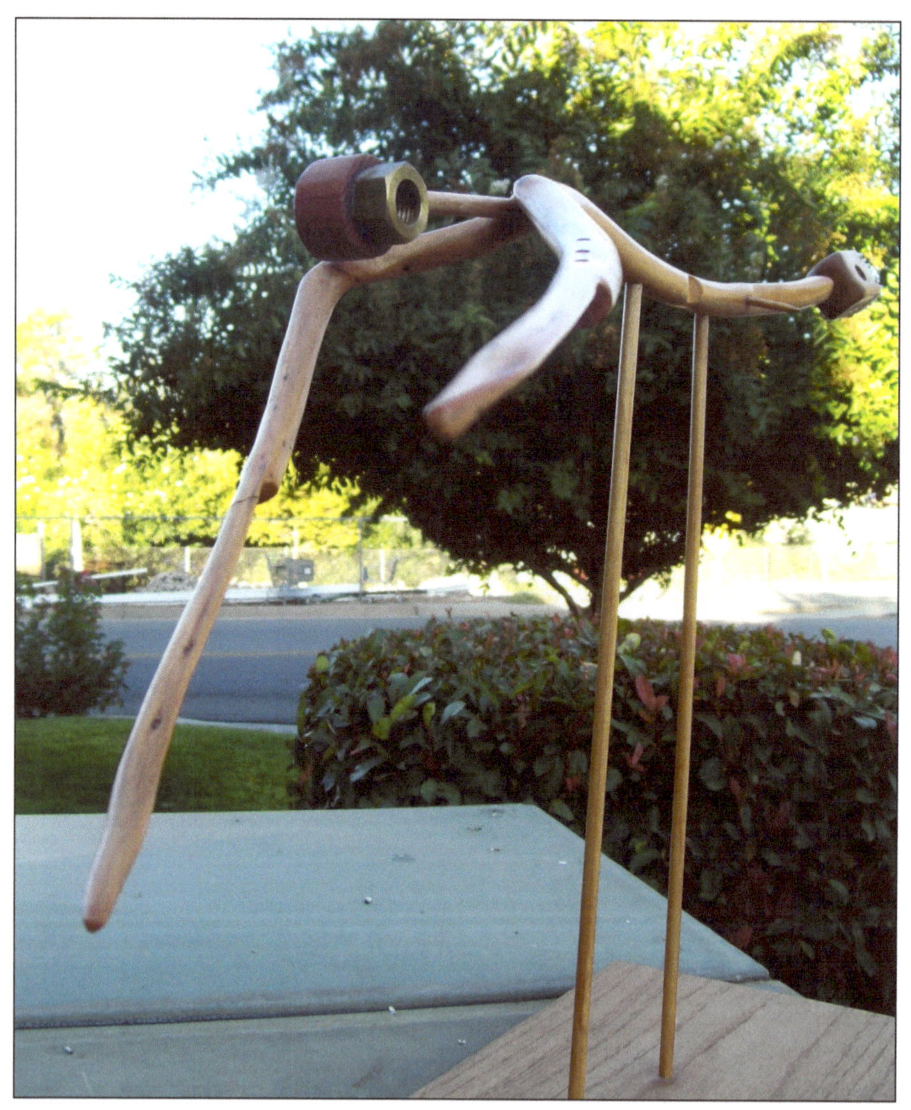

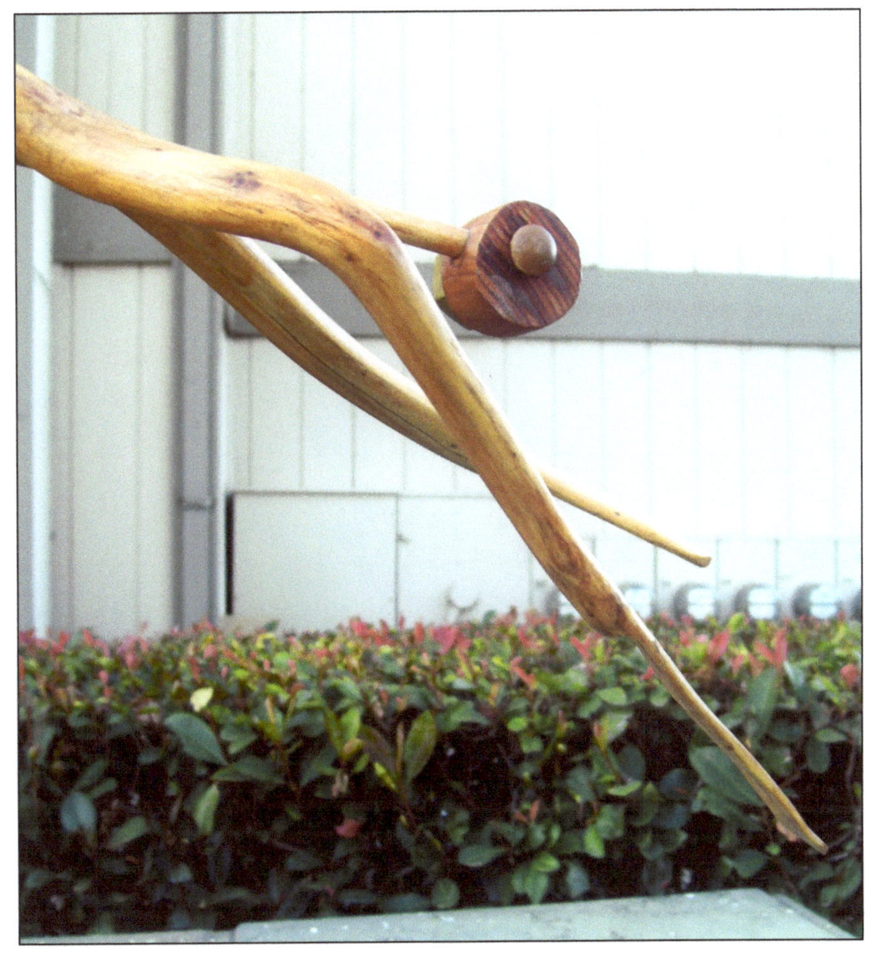

The Drugged Kid, mixed media, carved wood and found objects, 27" long (at left, and above)

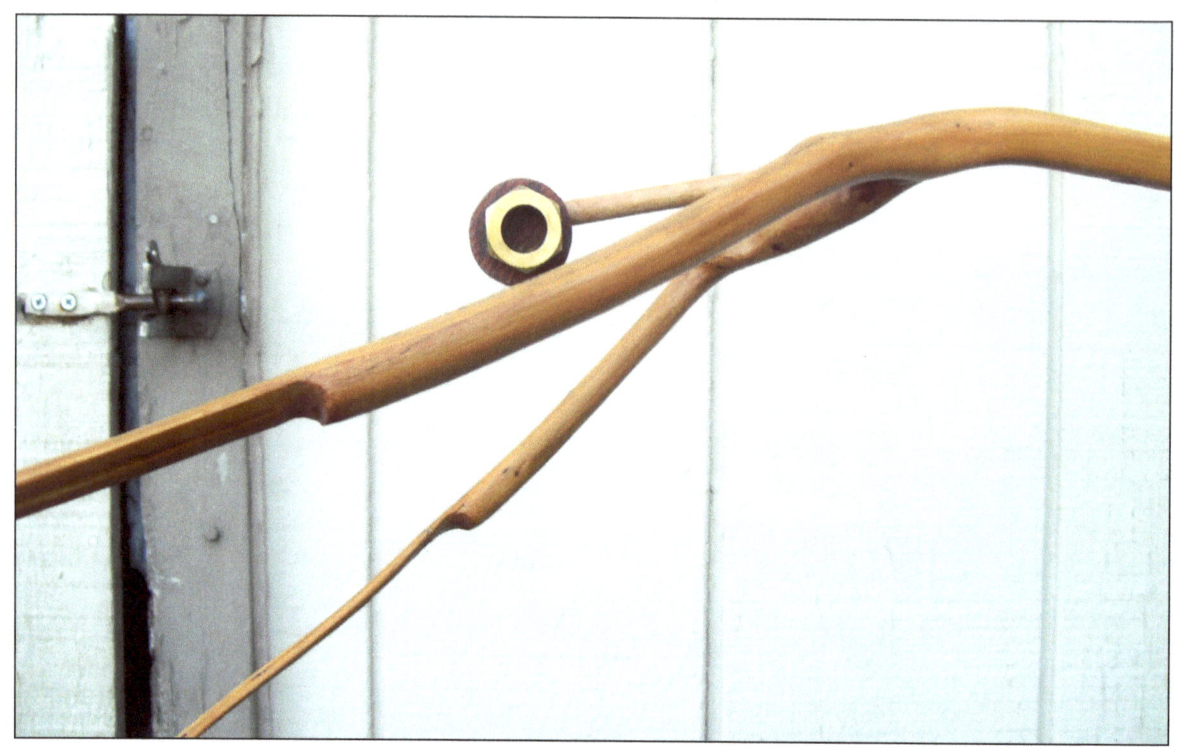

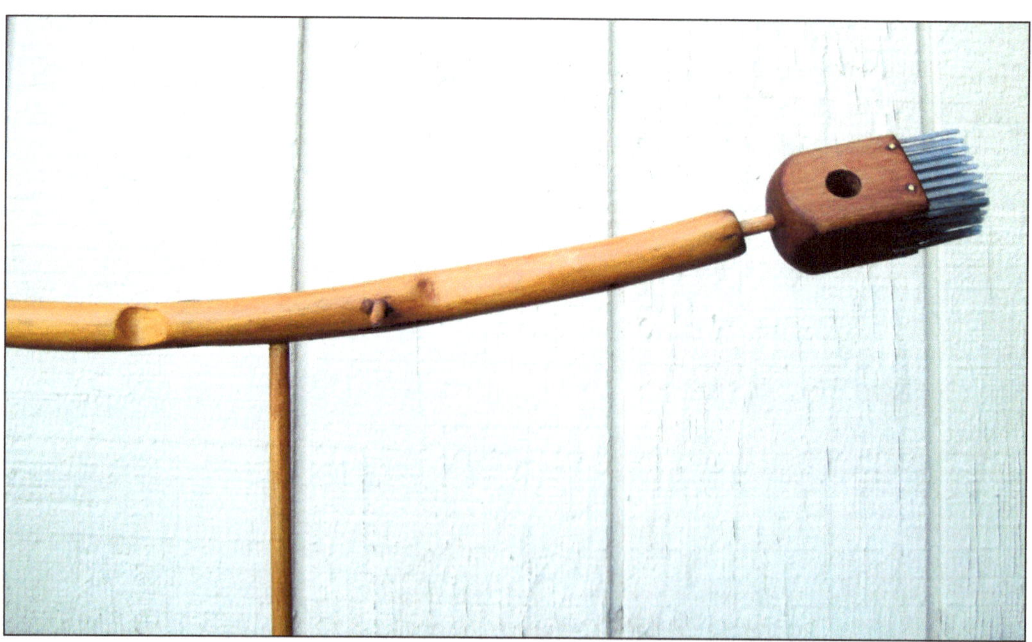

The Drugged Child, mixed media, carved wood and found objects, 27" long

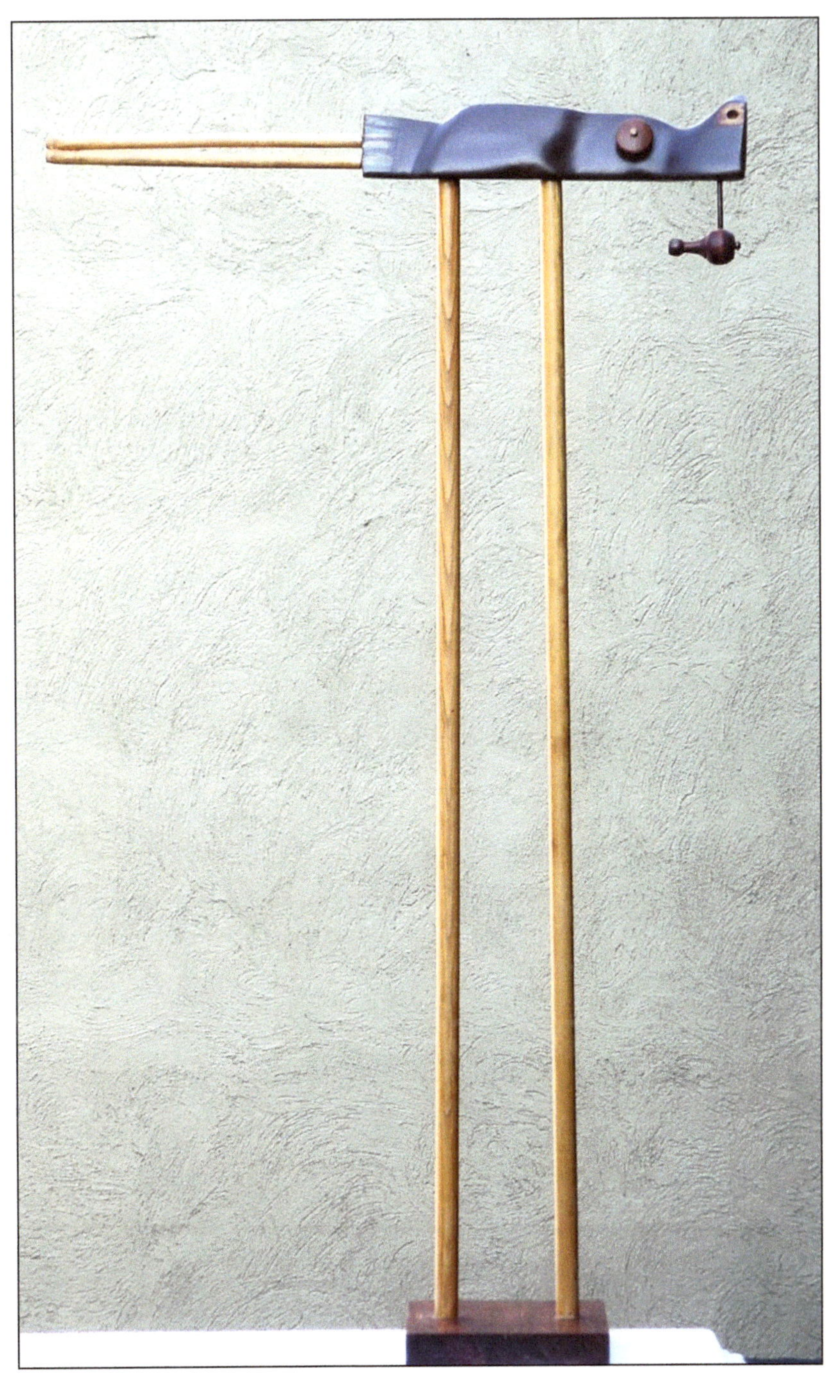

Nesting Bird and Baby, wood and found objects, 5 ft. 9" tall, 42" long

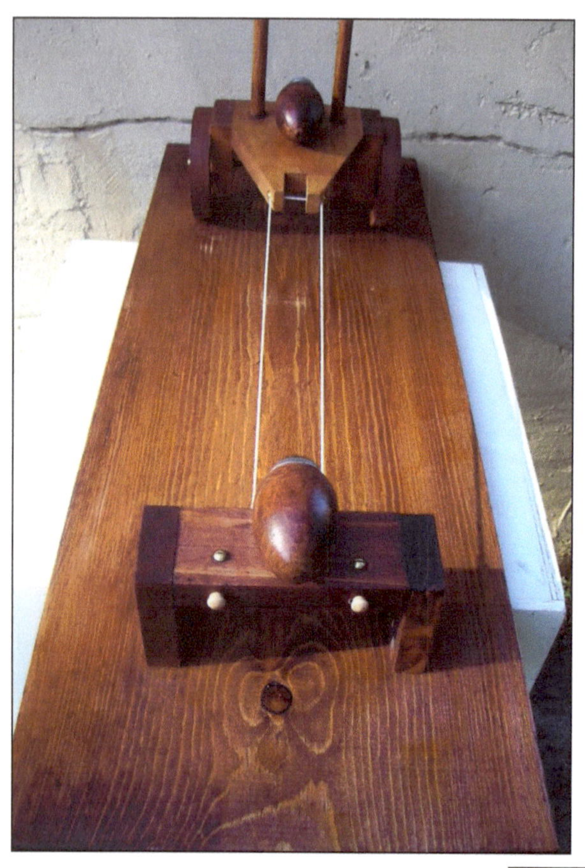

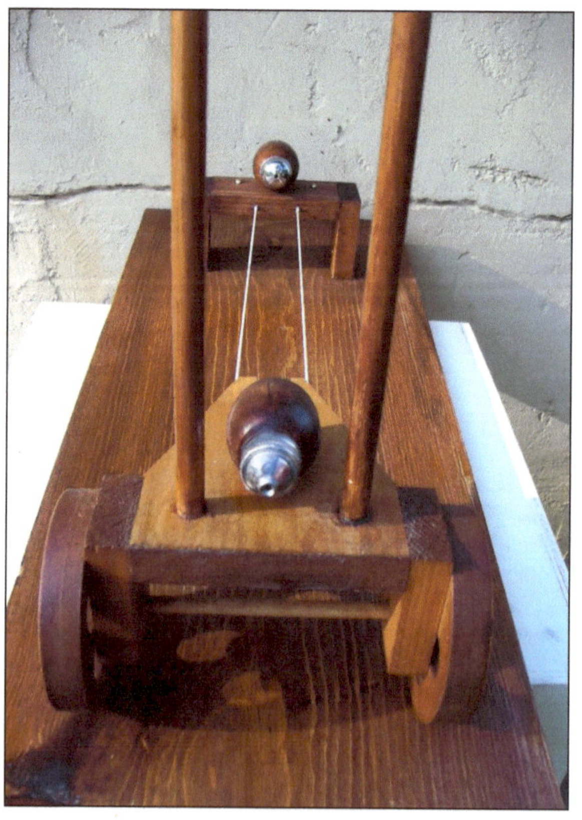

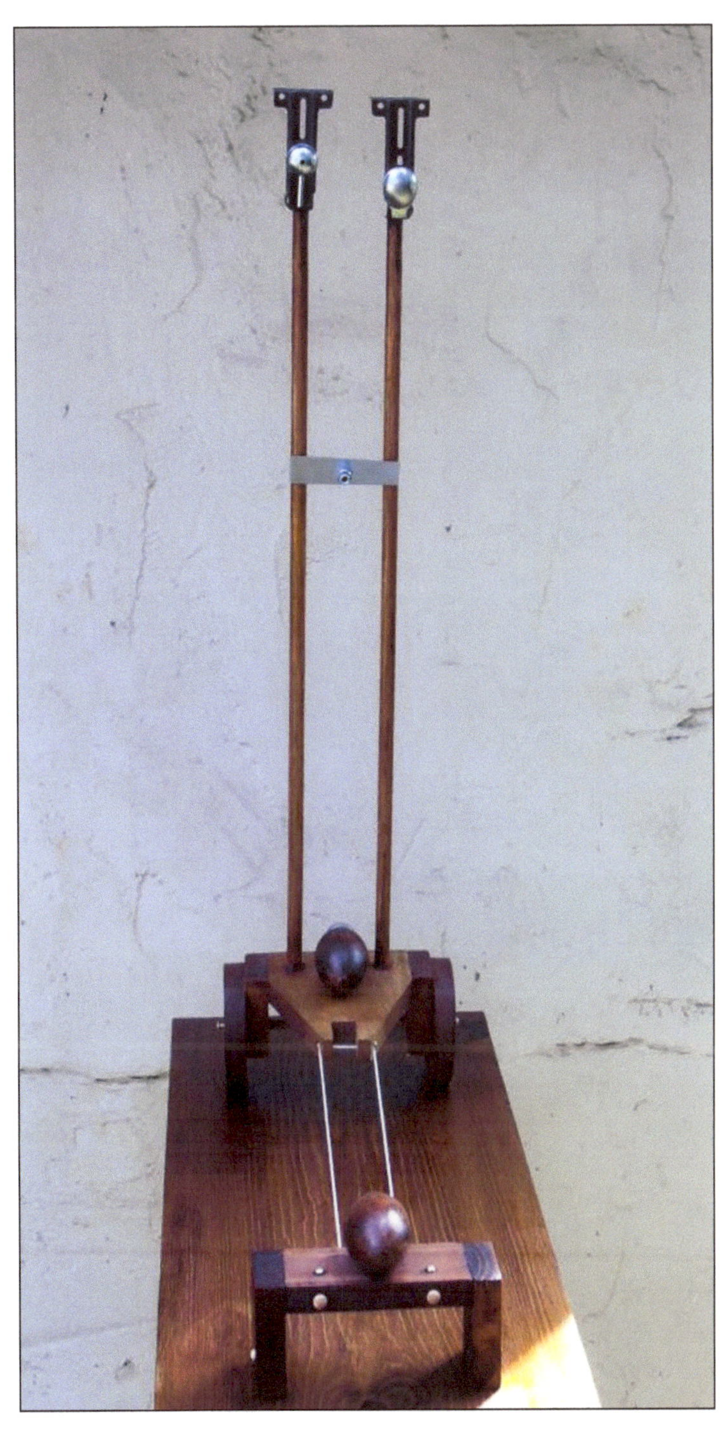

Codex Atlanticus - Da Vinci War Machine Designed to Fail (at left, and above)

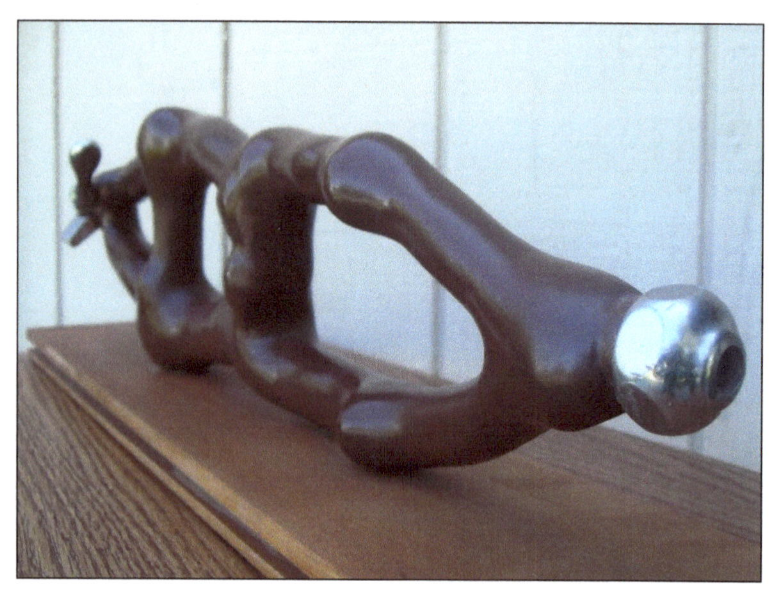

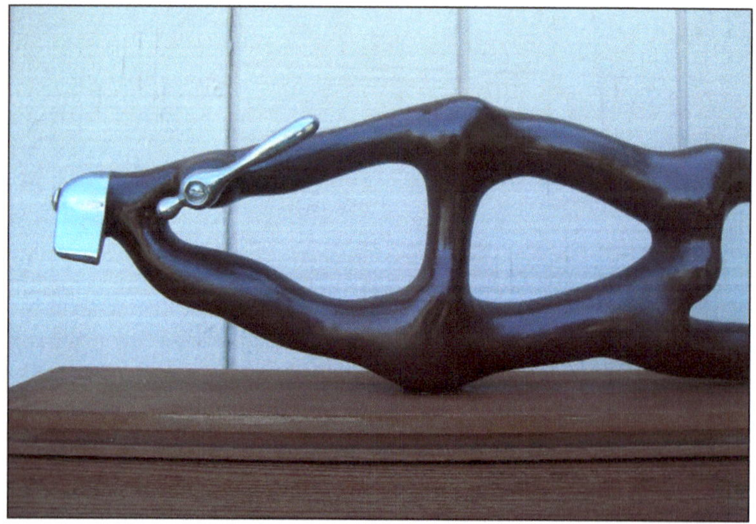

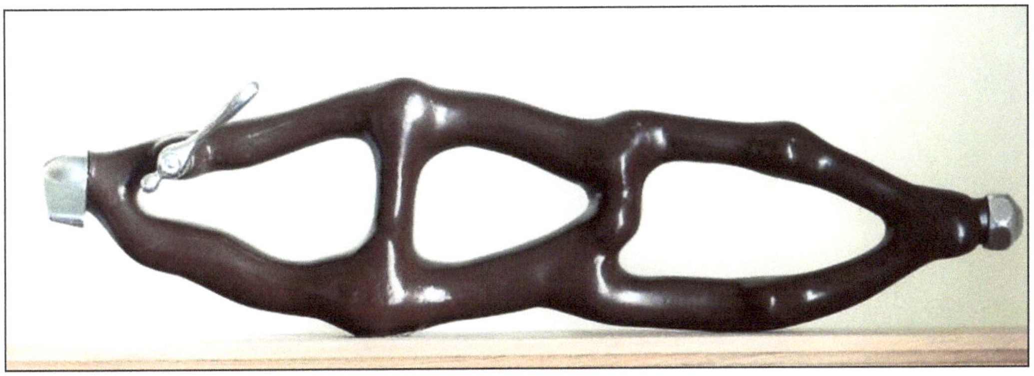

Flush Full Metal Jacket, fiberglass and chrome objects, 20" x 4" (at left, and above)

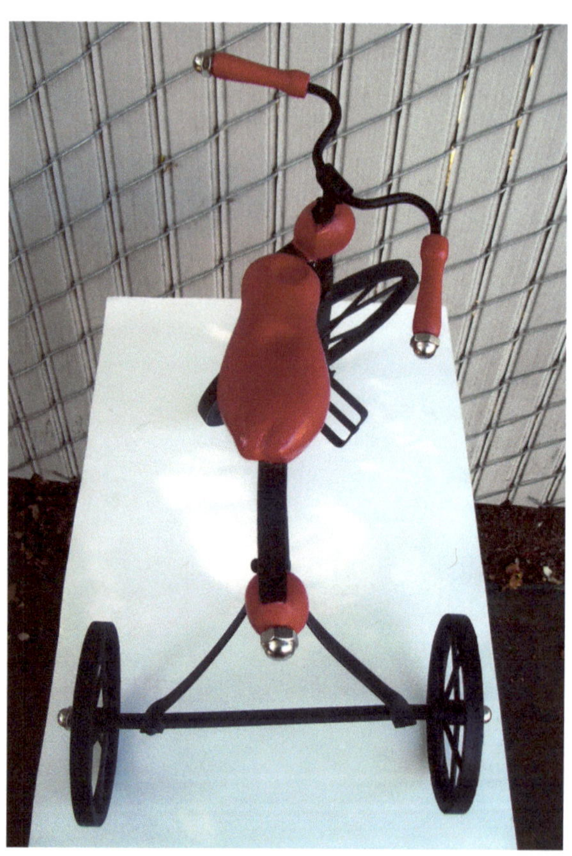

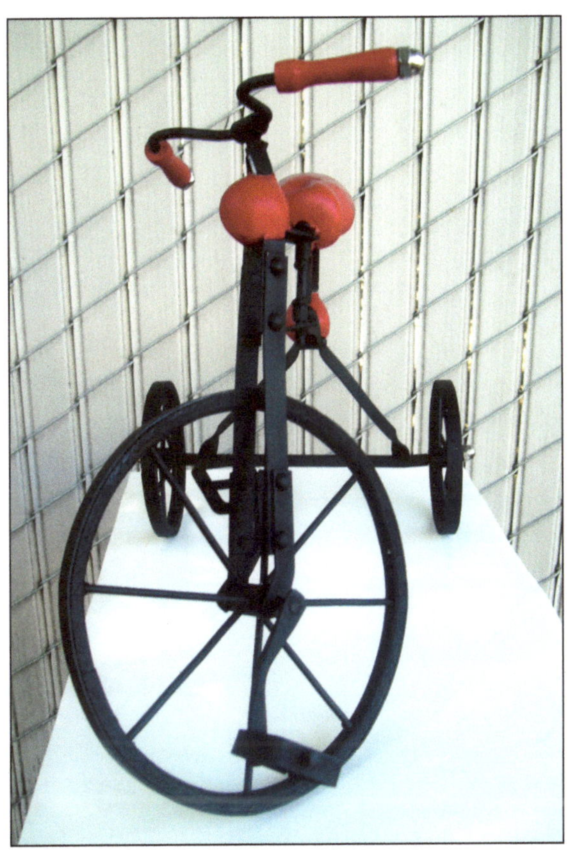

Red, forged iron, fiber glass, and stainless steel nuts and bolts, 18 x 13 x 10"(above, and at left)

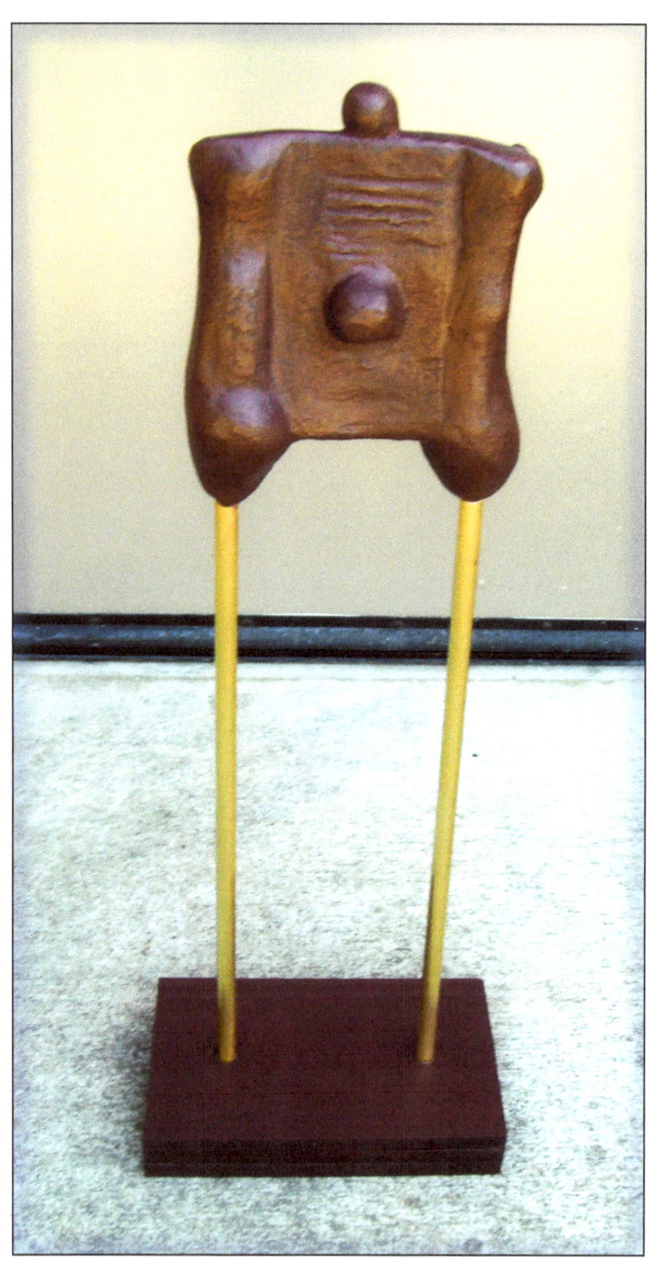

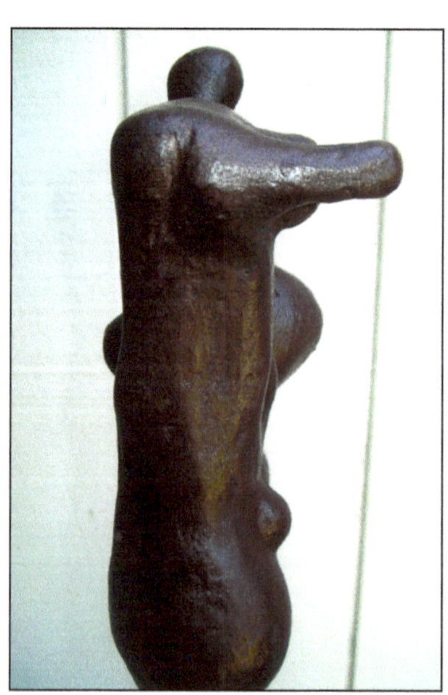

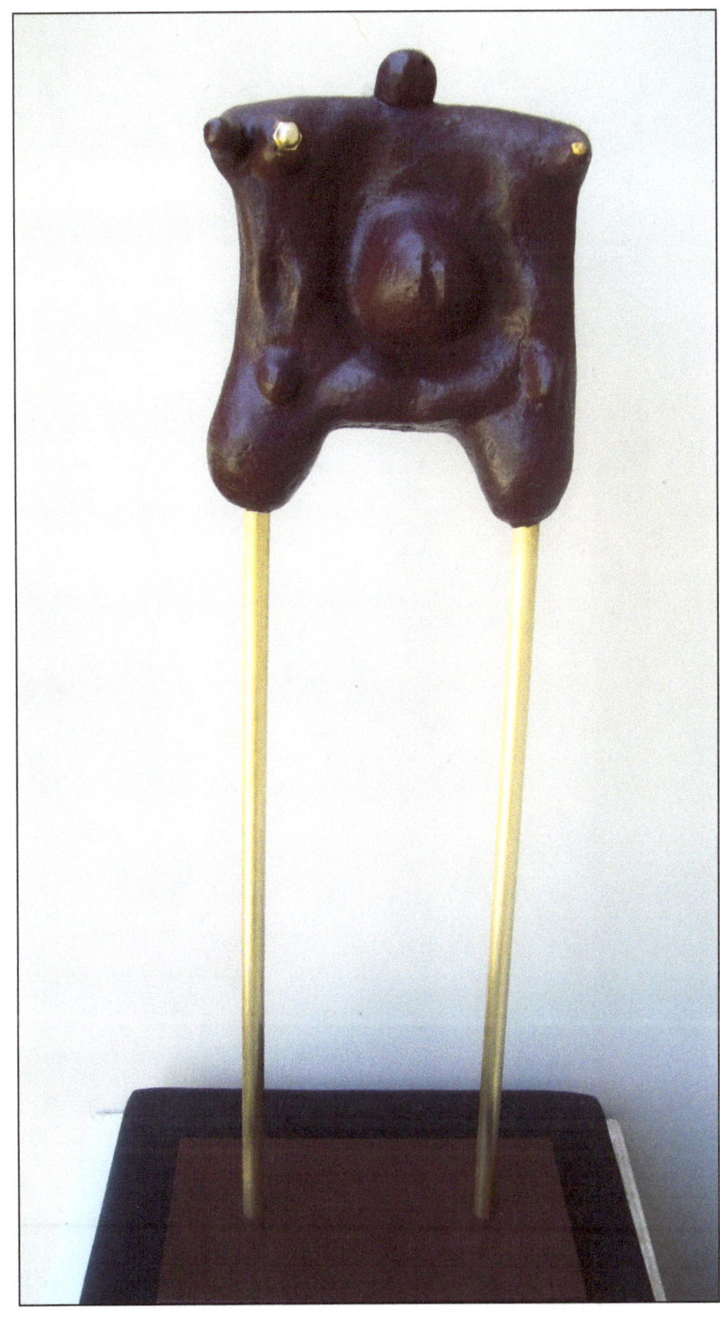

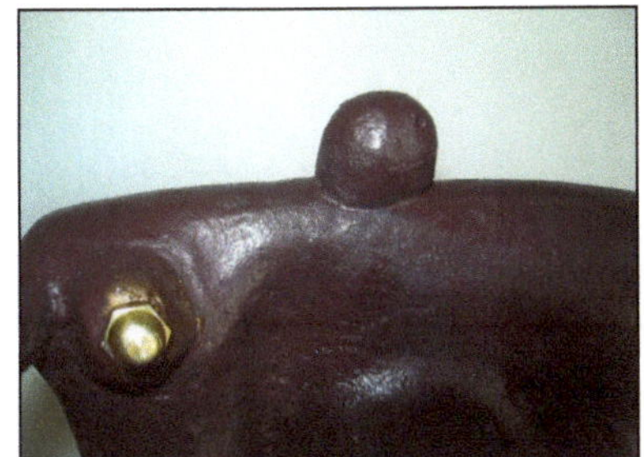

Lorenzo the Magnificent: Last of de Medici, model for a bronze edition of 10. The model is made of fiberglass and brass (at left, and above)

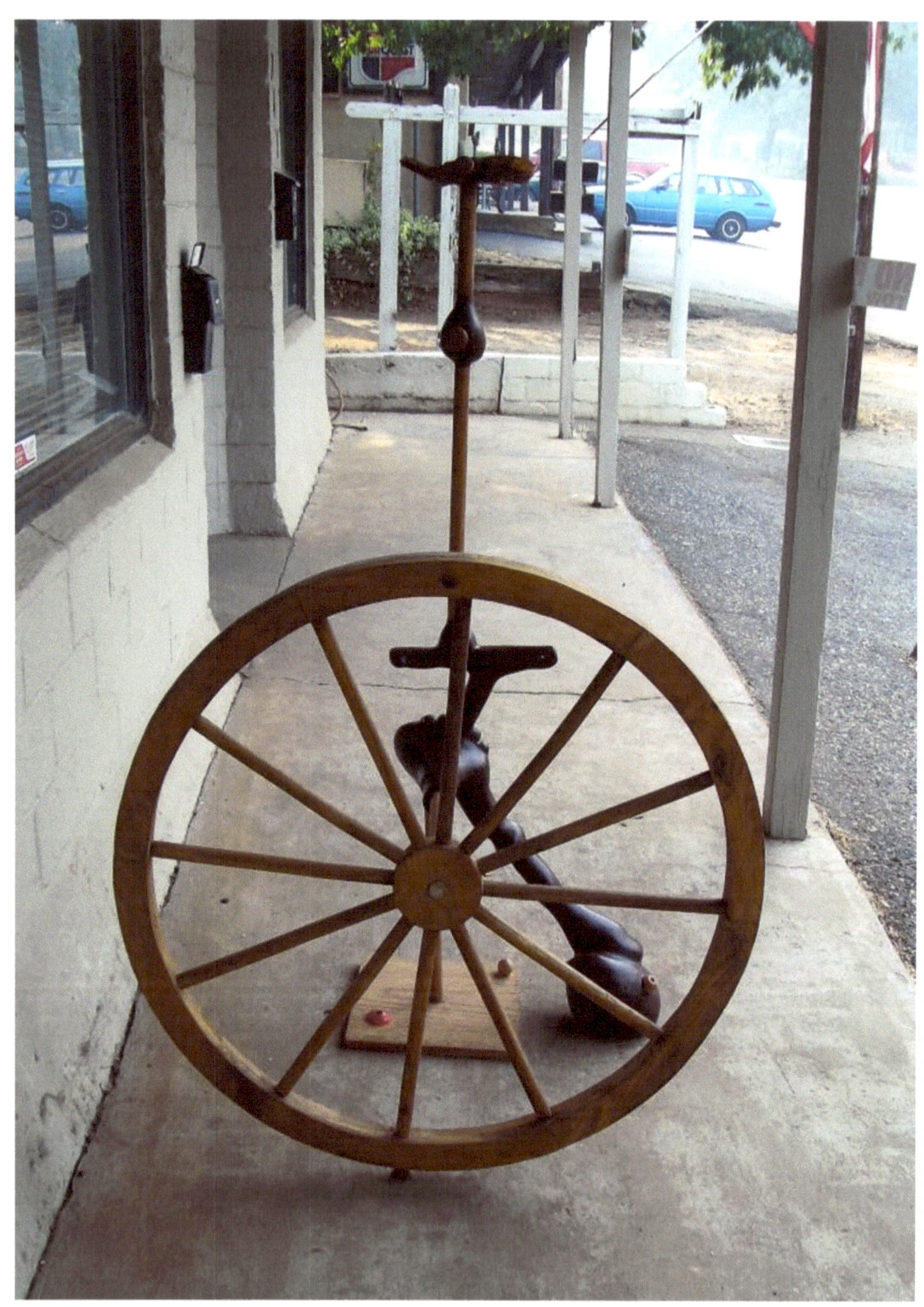

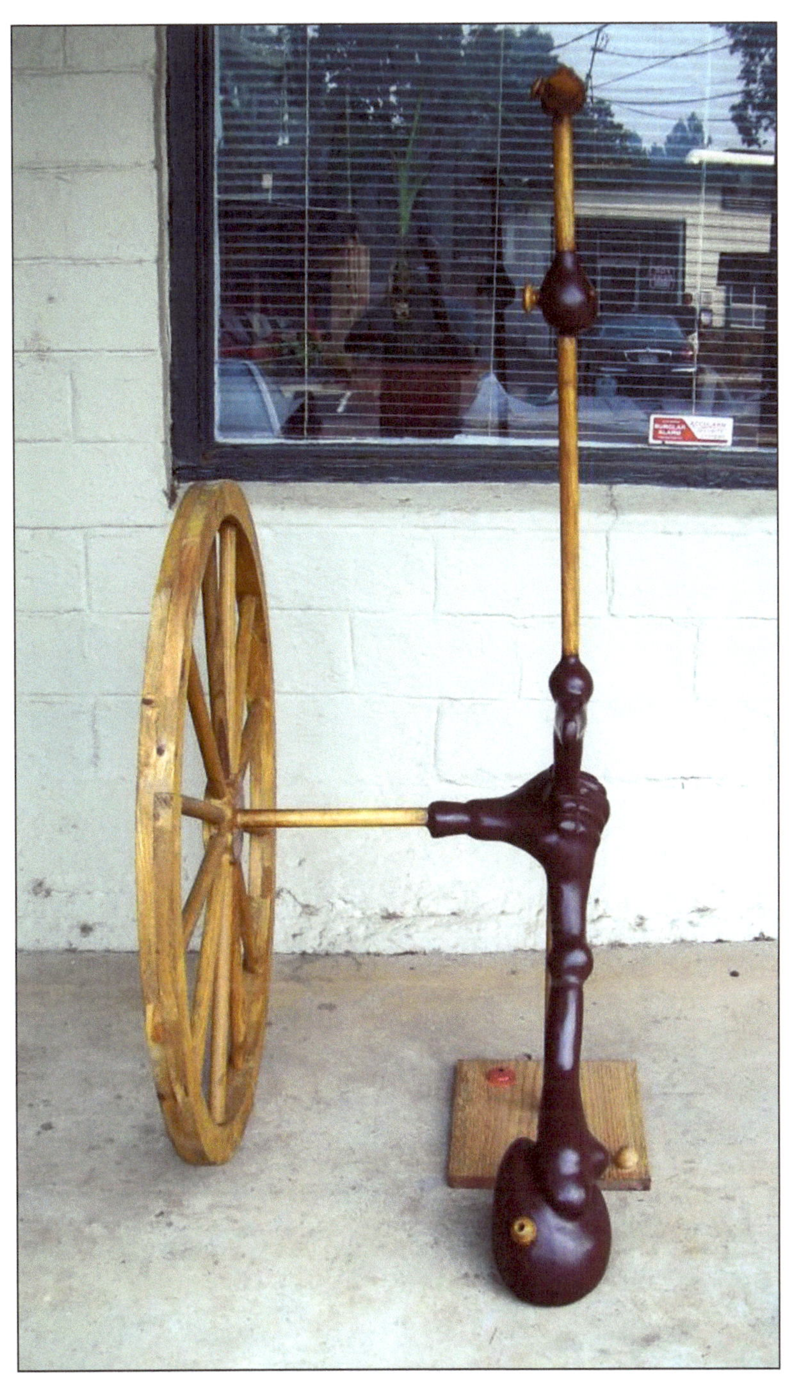

Big Foot and the Massacre at Wounded Knee, mixed media and found objects (at left, and above)

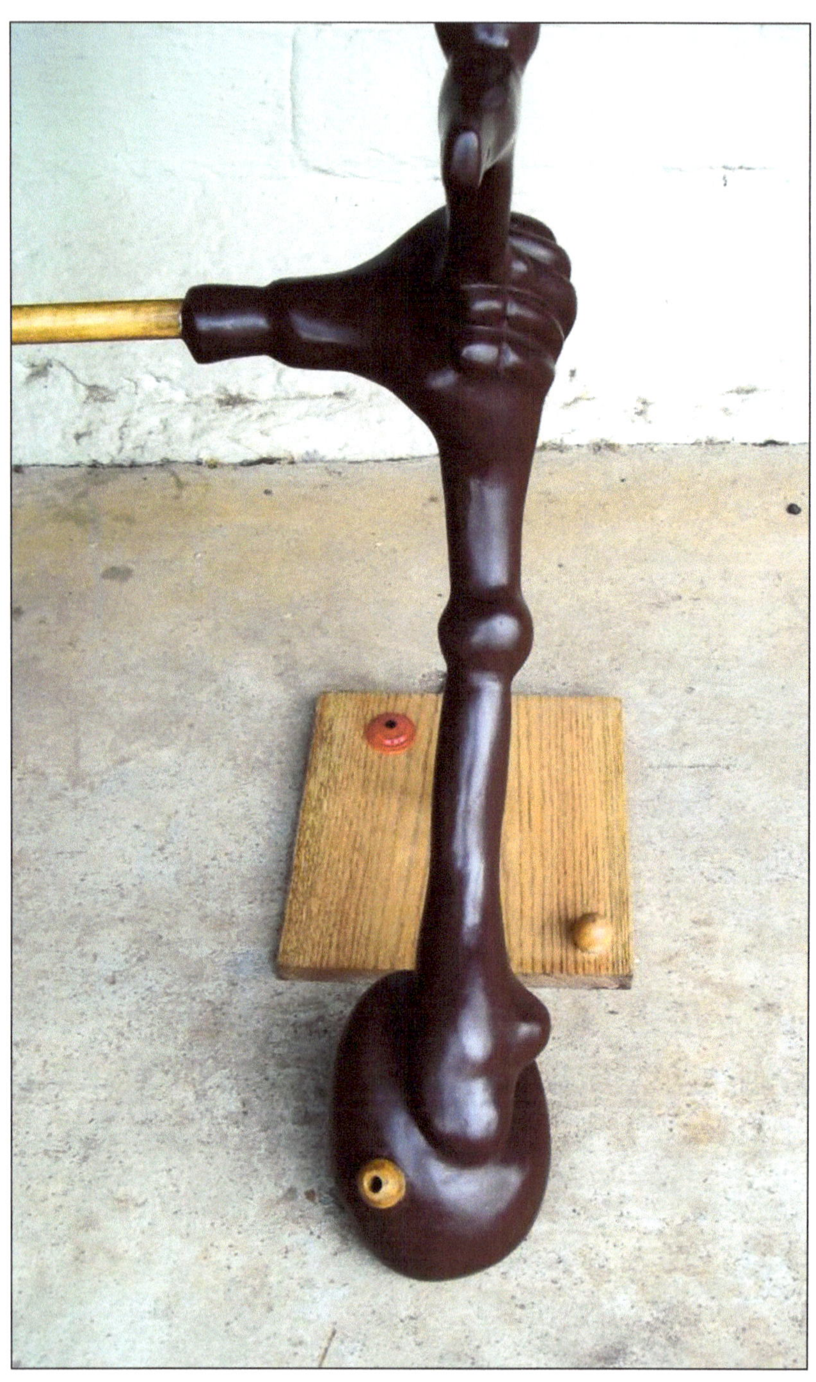

Big Foot and the Massacre at Wounded Knee, mixed media and found objects (at right, and above)

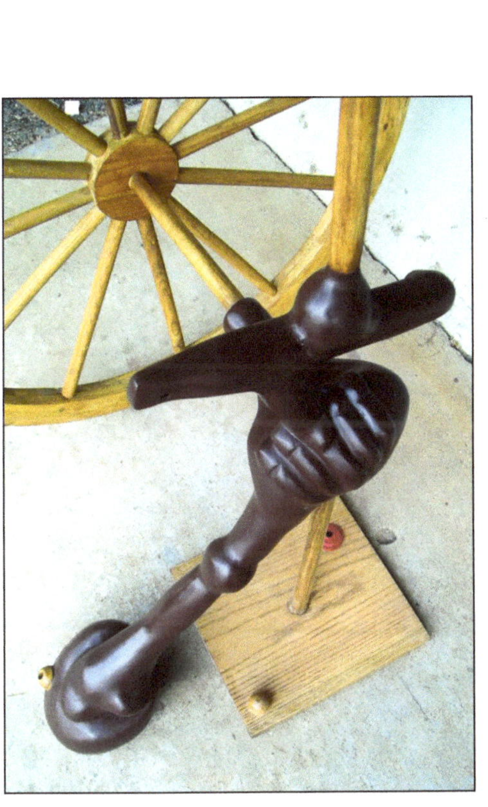

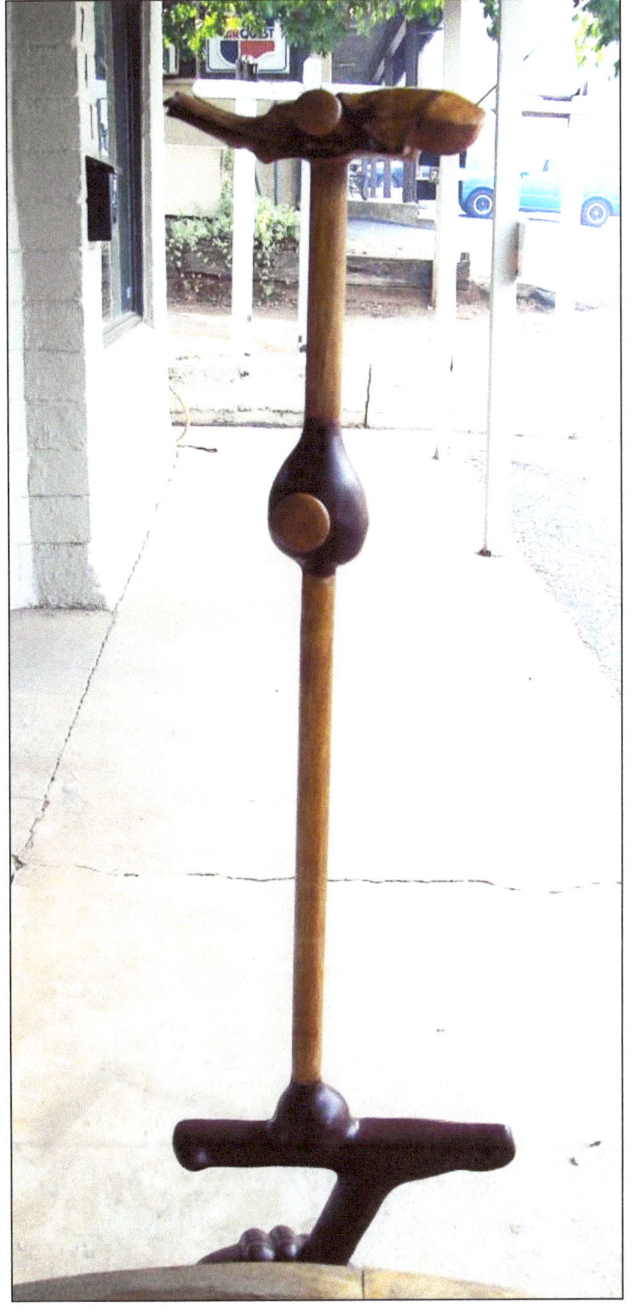

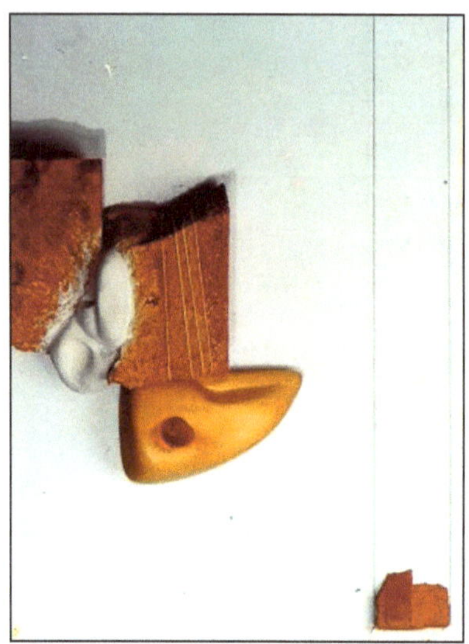

Death Valley, Swedish Tegel stone, plaster of Paris, wood, and string, 30" x 30" wall sculpture

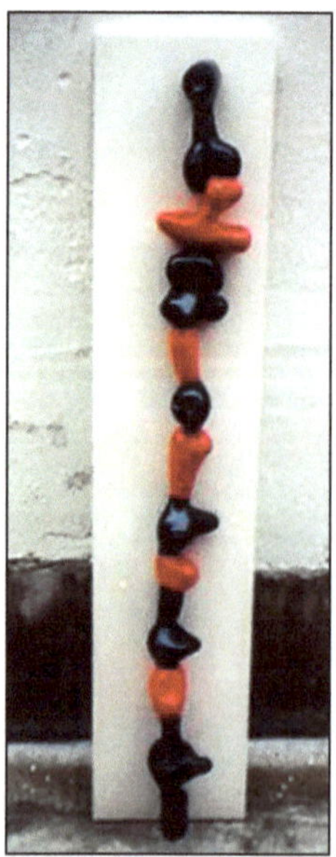

Mississippi Burning, fiberglass over clay, 5 ft. long wall sculpture

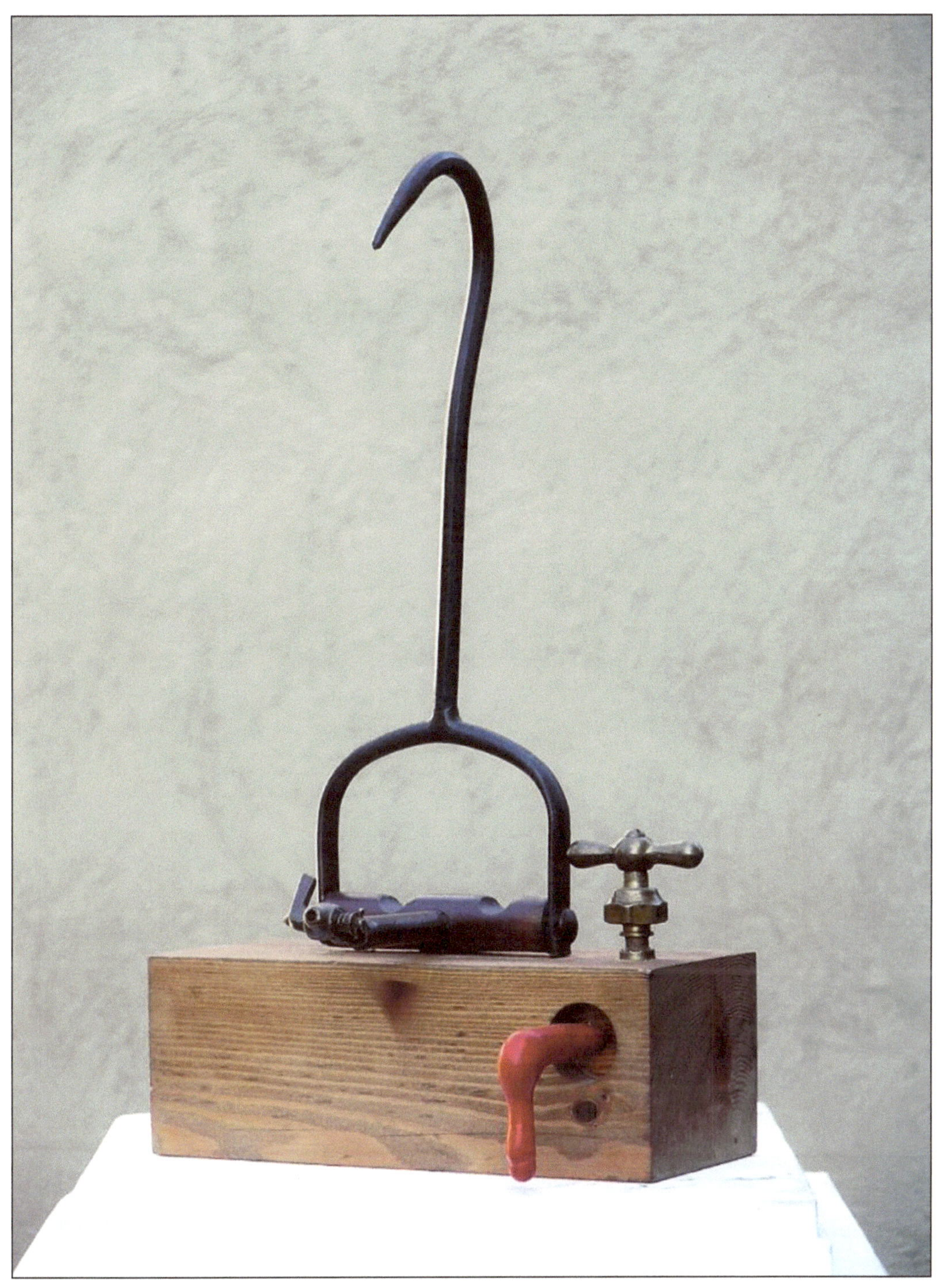

Exxon Oil King, found objects, wood, iron, and fiber glass. This sculpture represents Harris' vision of the corporate oil barons who are squeezing blood from the consumers. The tap is continuously turned on.

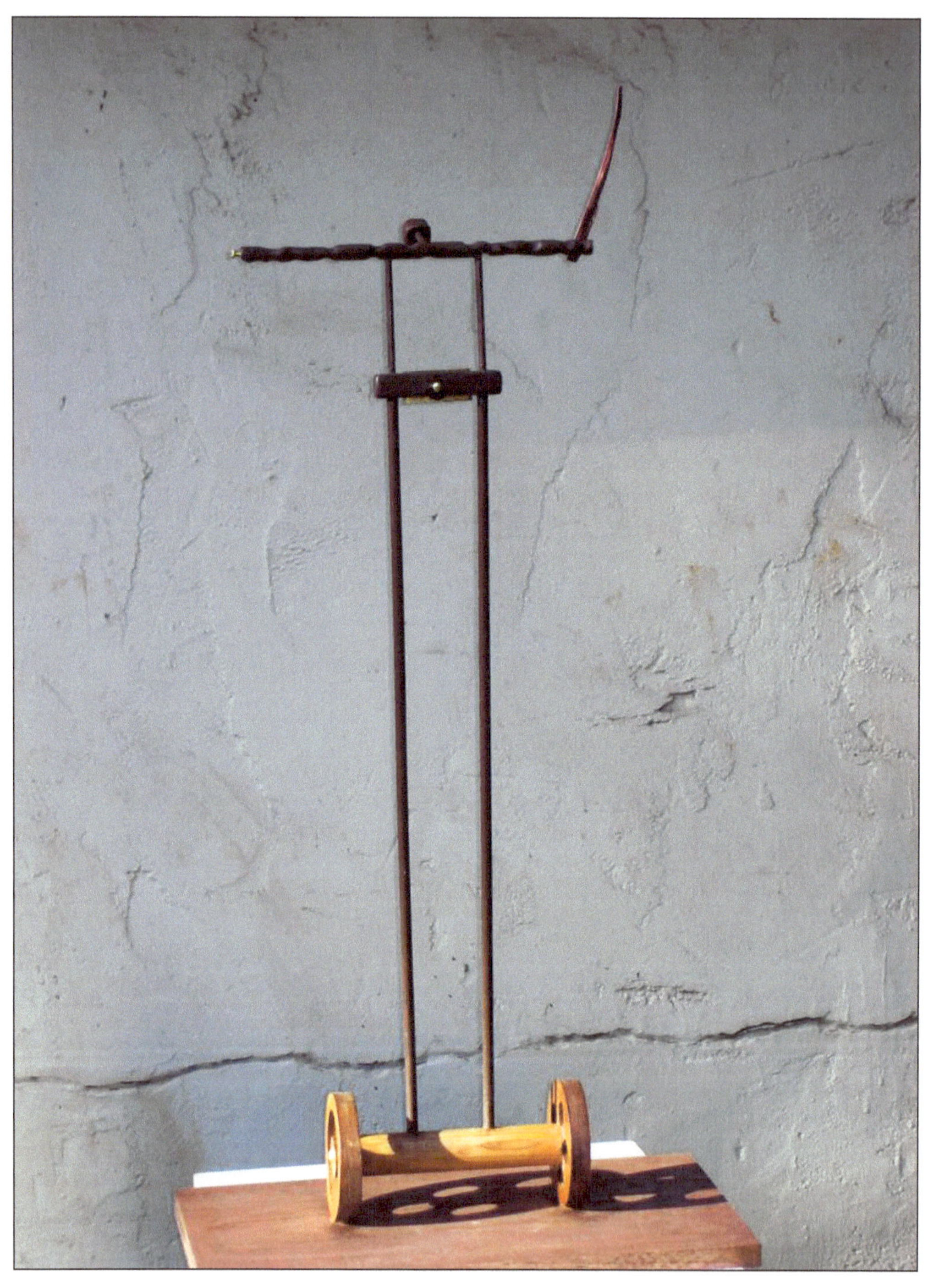

Skinhead Fly Boy, wood and mixed media, 36" high (above, and close-up at right)

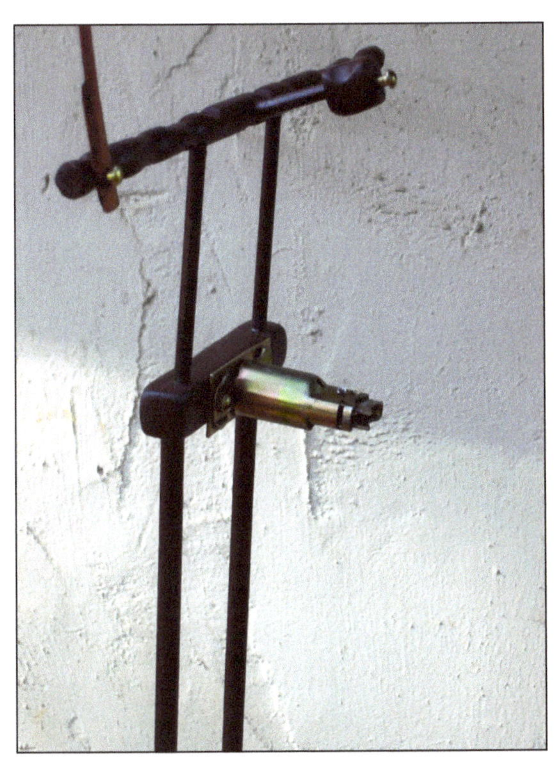

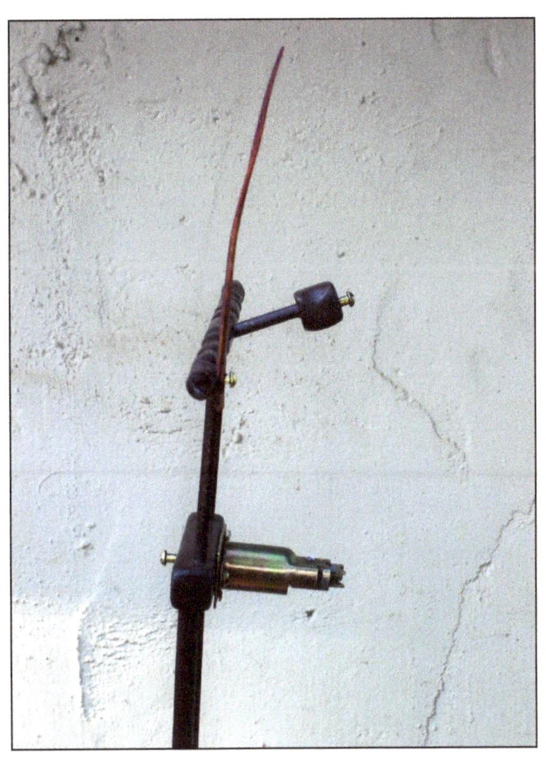

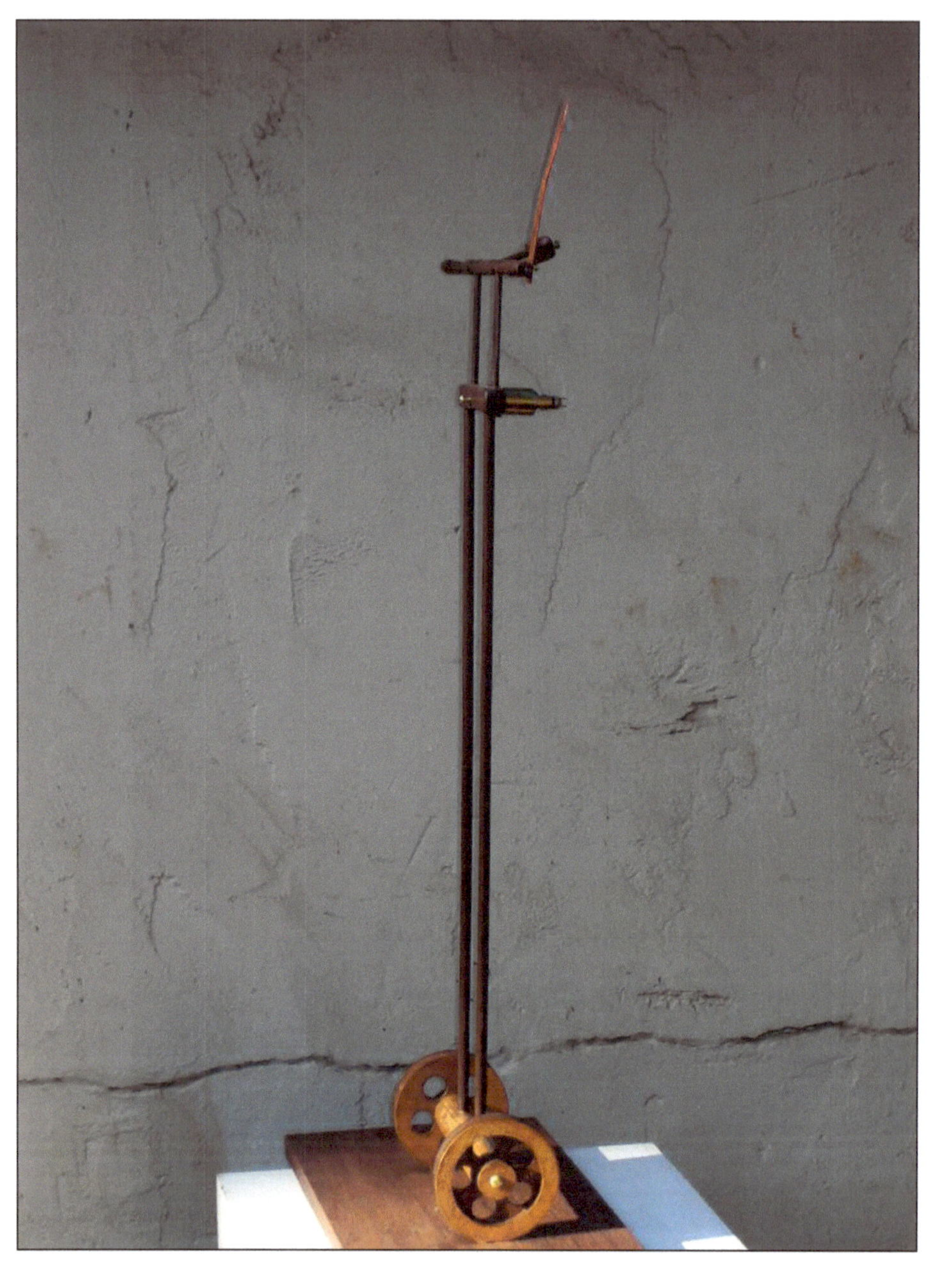

Skinhead Fly Boy, wood and mixed media, 36" high

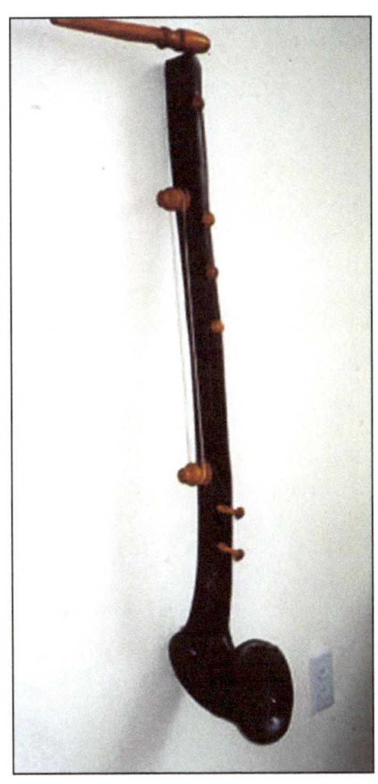

Homage to Charlie Parker, carved wood, string, found objects, laminated clay, and knobs, 5 ft. 5" wall sculpture

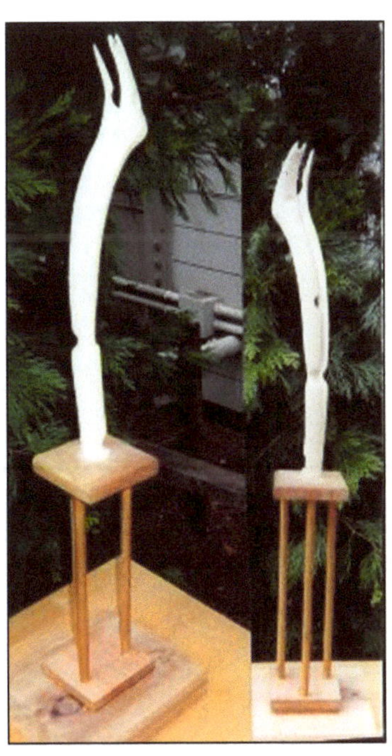

Two figures standing on the tower of Babel, carved Oregon white pine, and found wood pedestal, 18" high

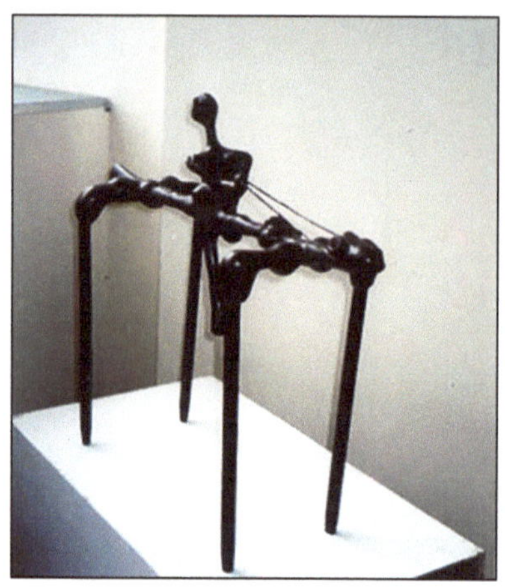

Wounded Warrior, laminated clay (bondo), wood, and leather. 36" x 42"

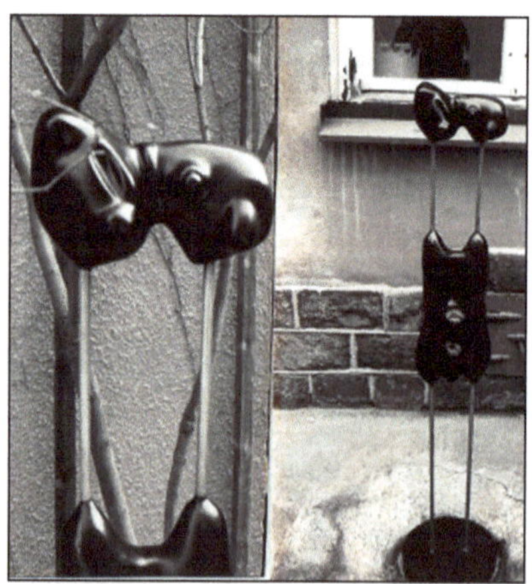

Double Standing Figure, cast resin and steel, 5 ft. tall

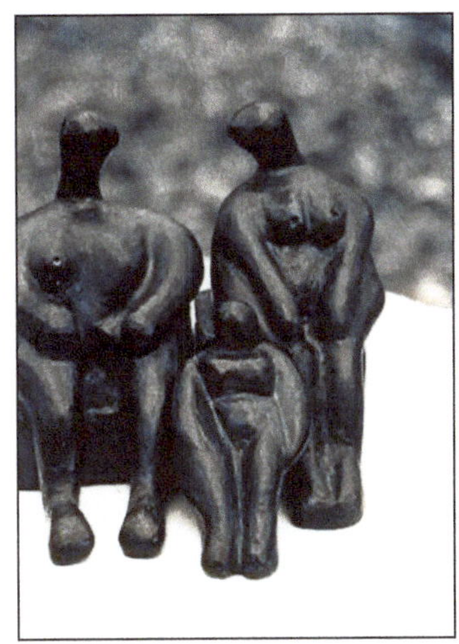

Family: Homage to Britt-Marie Harris, laminated clay (bondo)

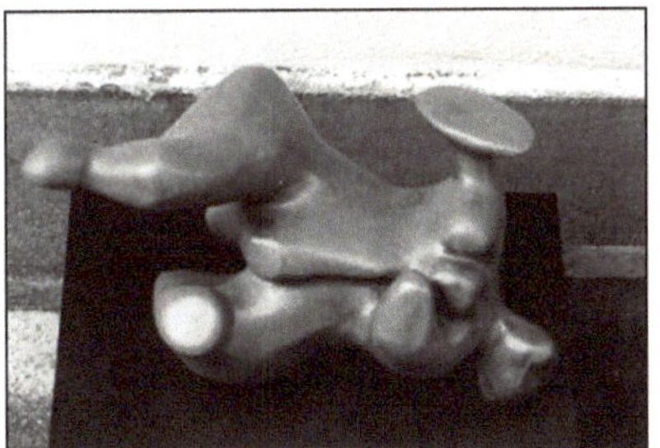

Reclining warrior: homage to Henry Moore-1, 24" x 10" bronze

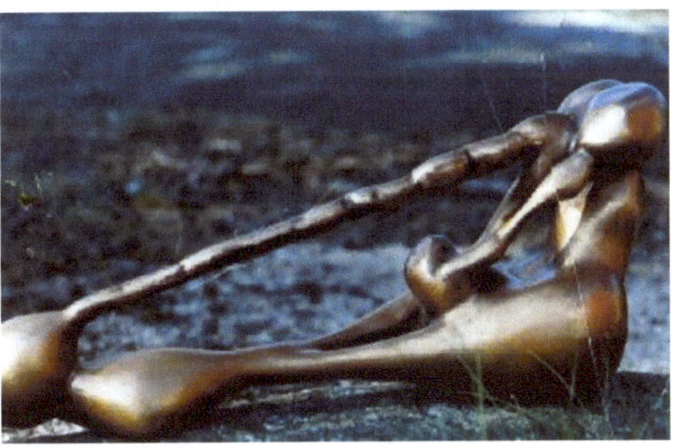

Struggling Forms: Homage to Henry Moore, bronze sculpture

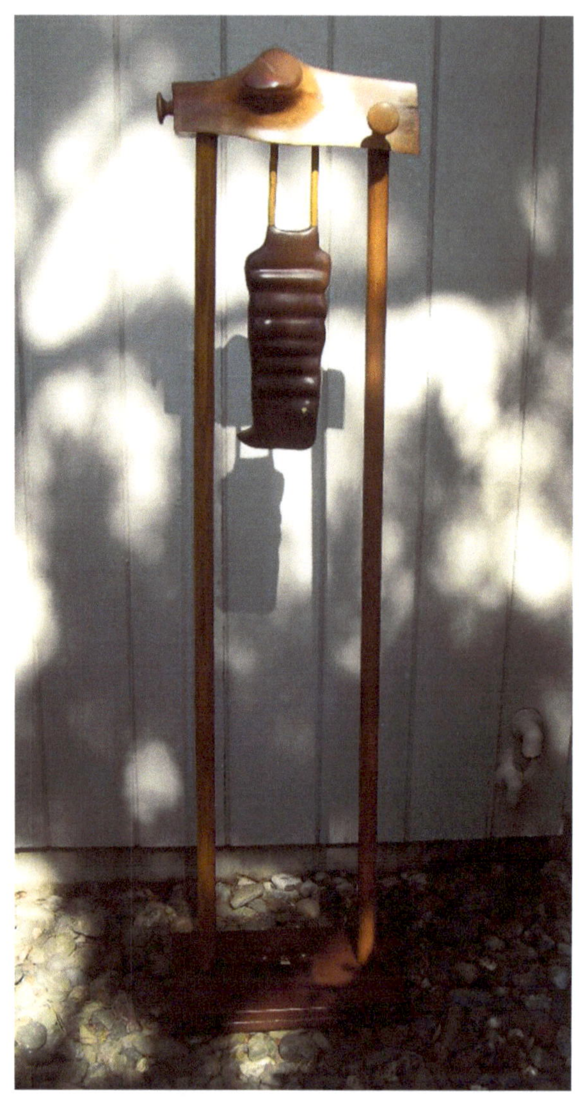

Headless Roman Centurion, carved wood, dowels, door knobs, fiber glass (bondo over clay). on the bottom of the base is a square block of wood with brass fixtures and screws (above, and close-ups at right)

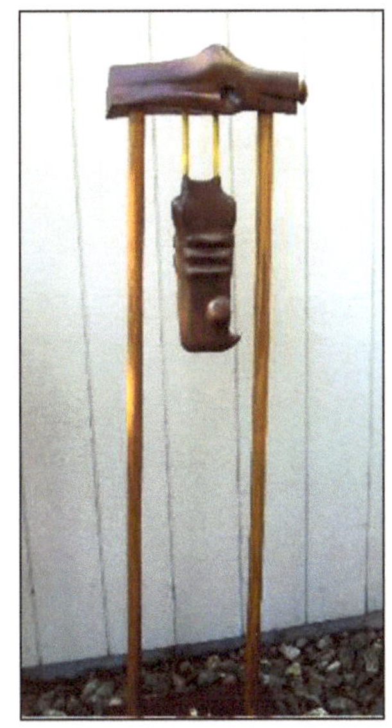

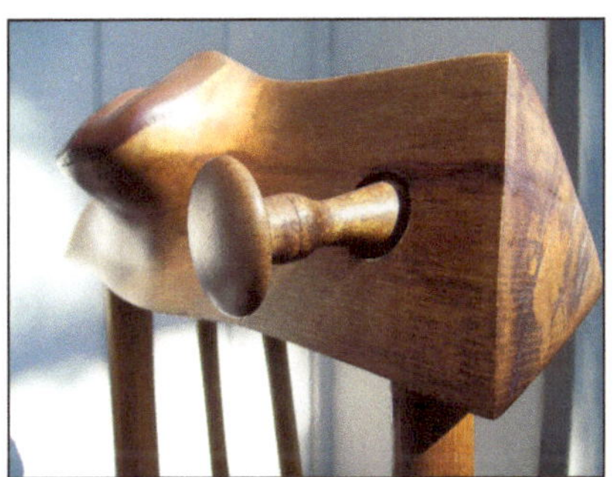

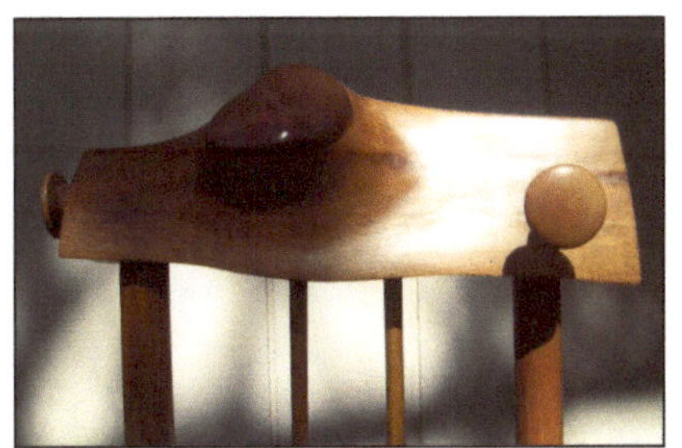

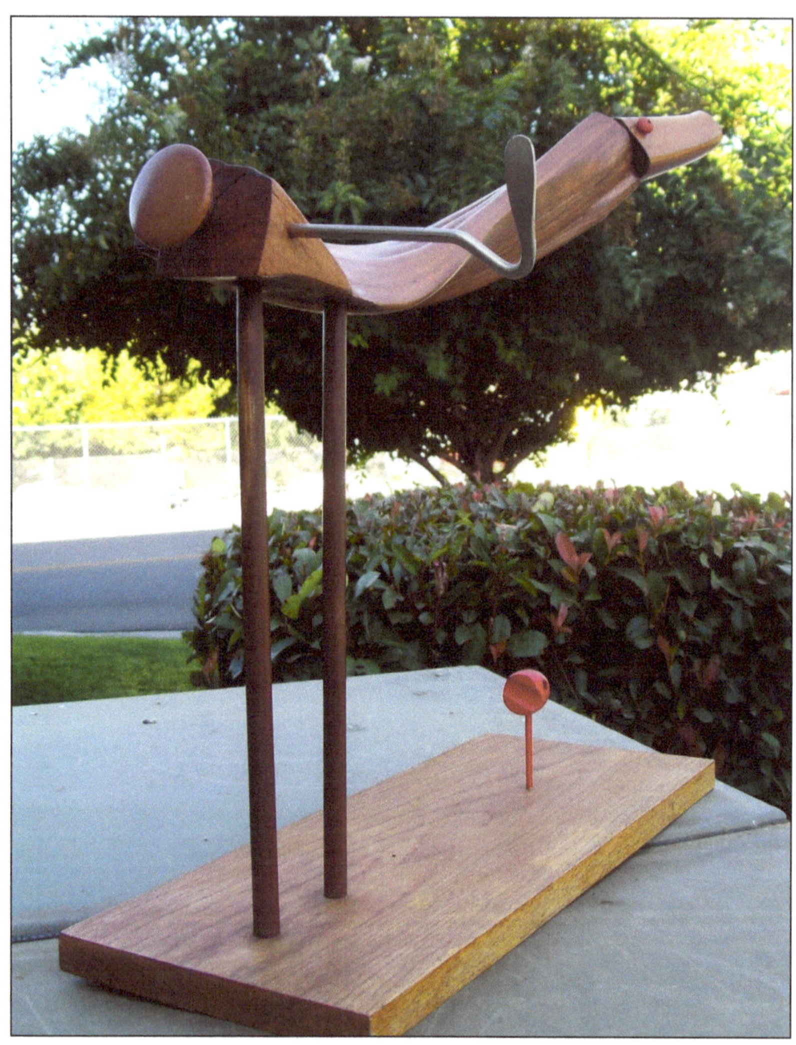

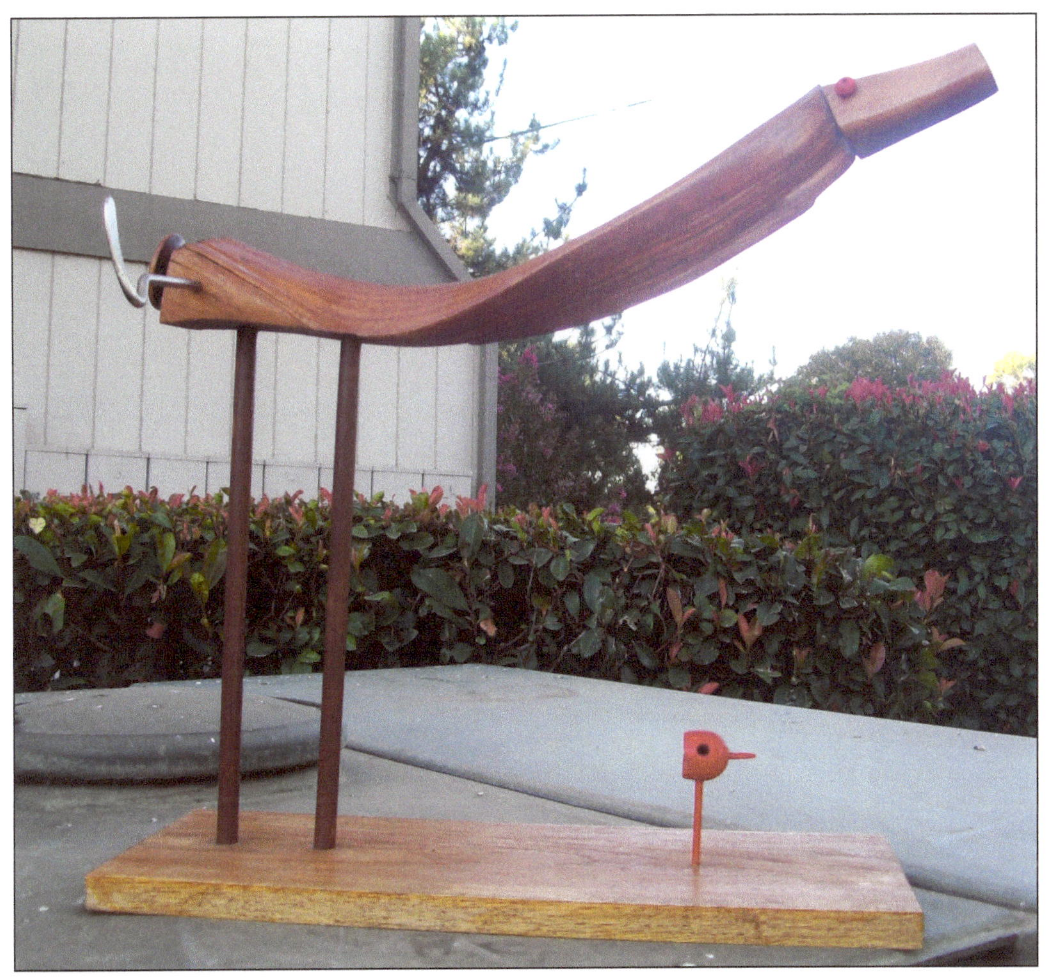

Balinese Fighting Cock, carved wood and found objects, 17" x 24" (at left, and above)

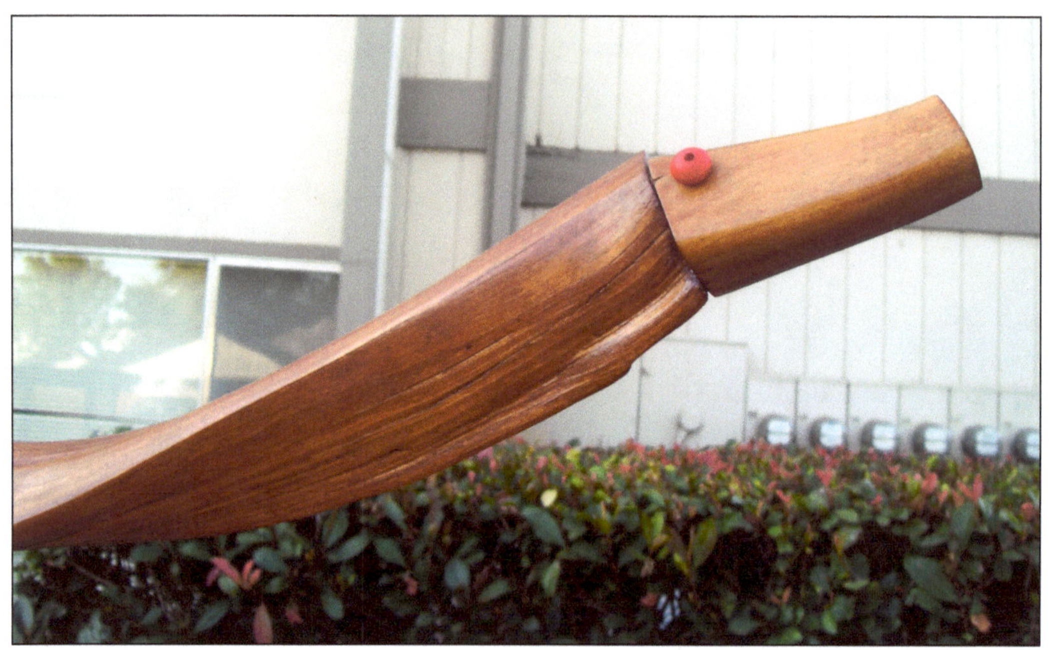

Balinese Fighting Cock, carved wood and found objects, 17" x 24" (close-up)

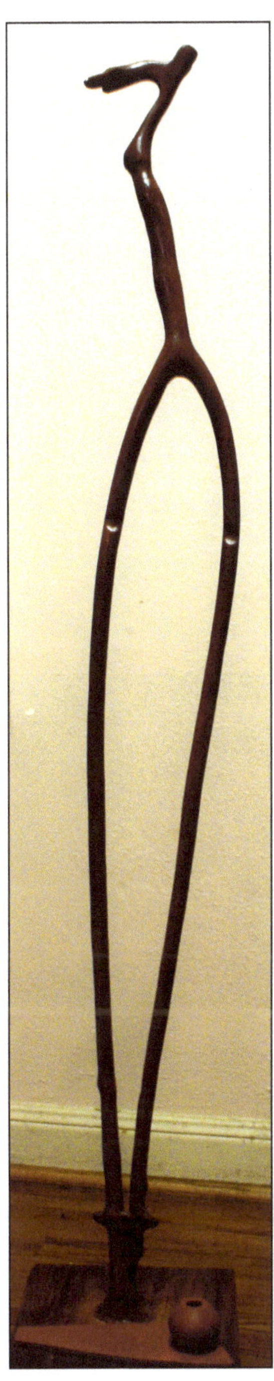

Isidora Duncan, found wood, 11" tall including base

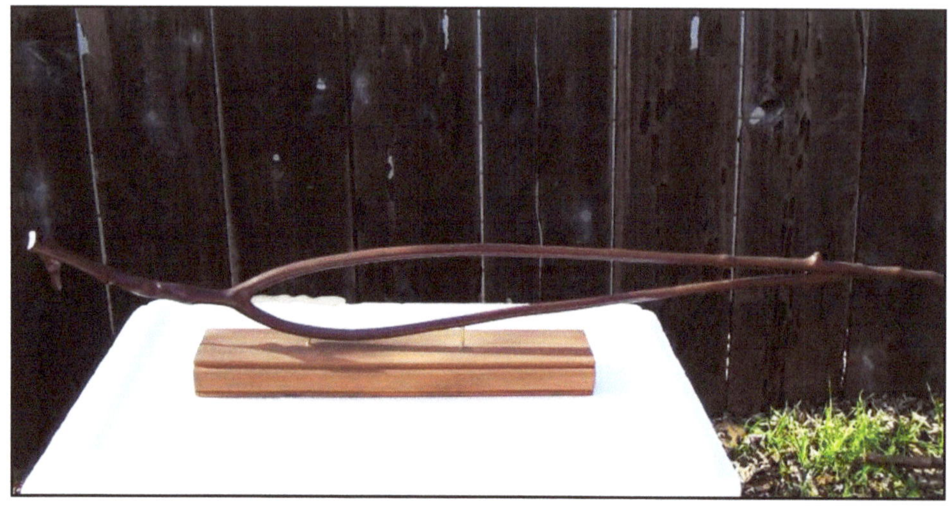

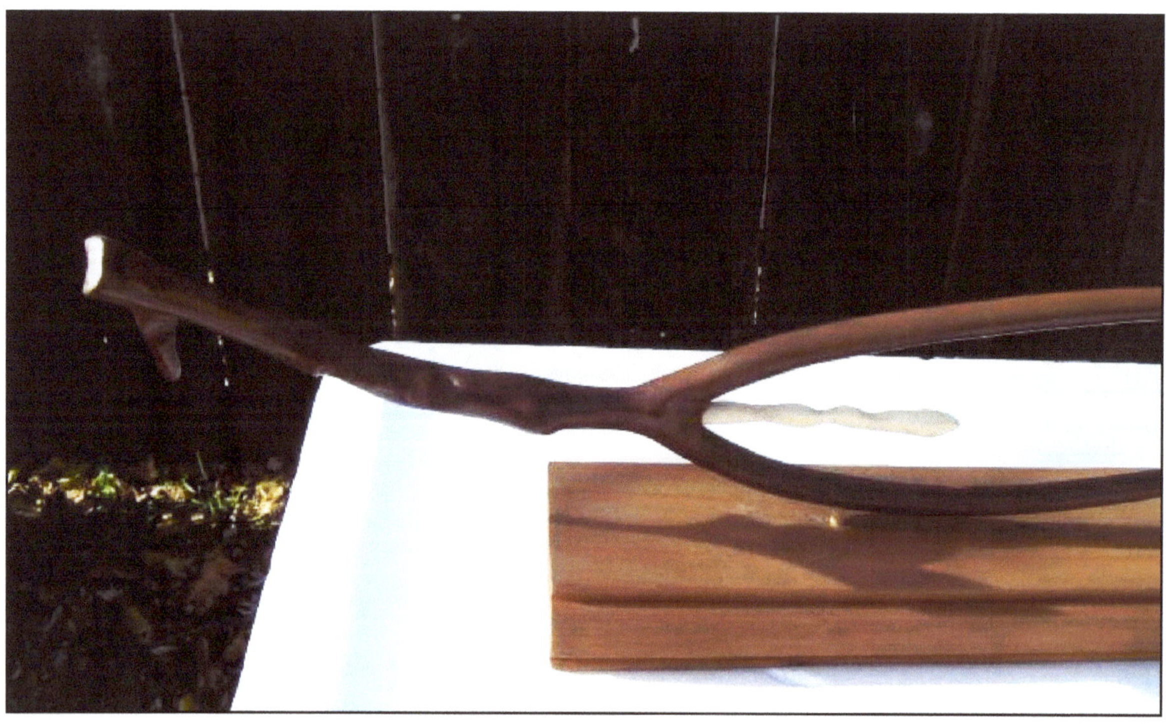

Nagasaki Nightmare/ Memento Mori, carved and painted wood, 32" long

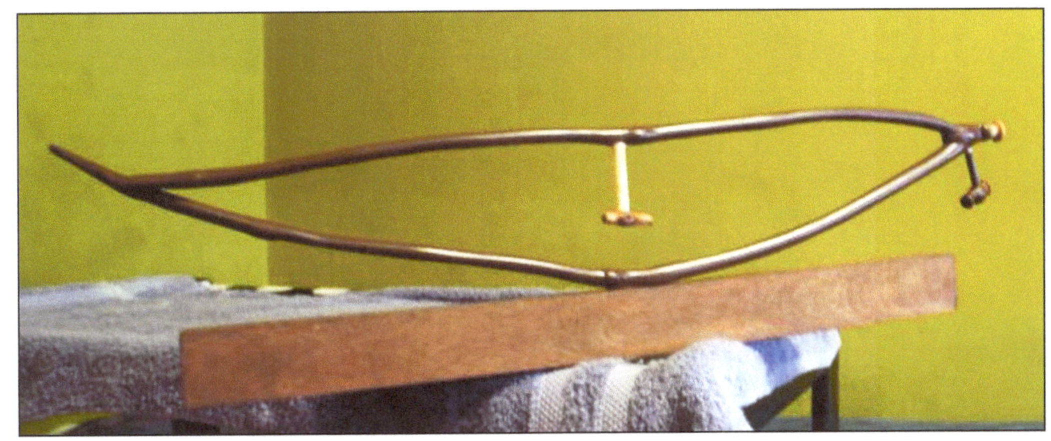

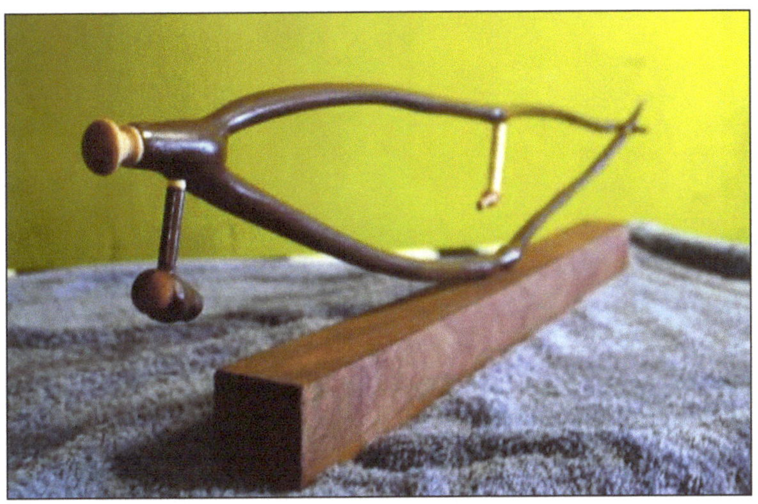

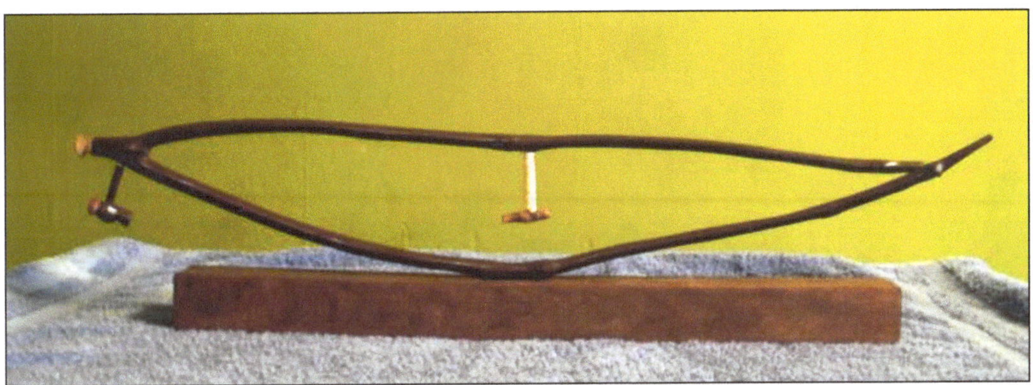

Remember Wounded Knee, wood, string, and found objects, 34" long

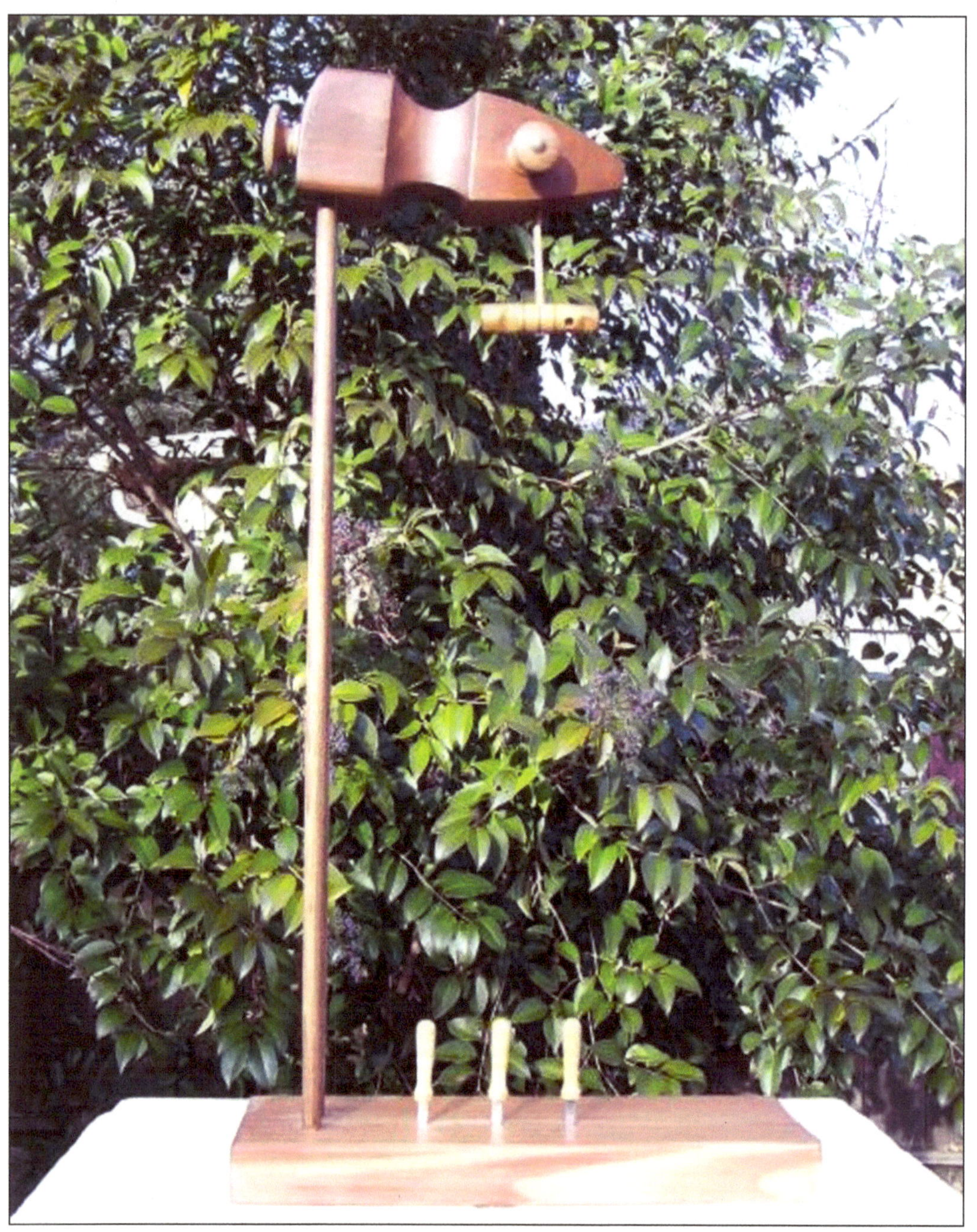

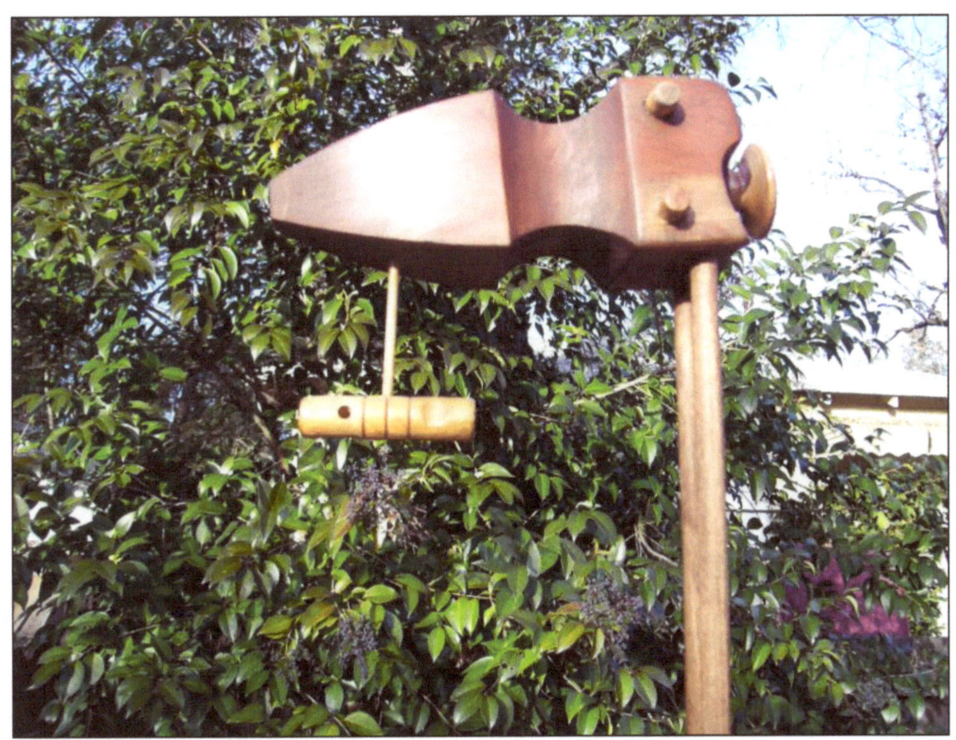

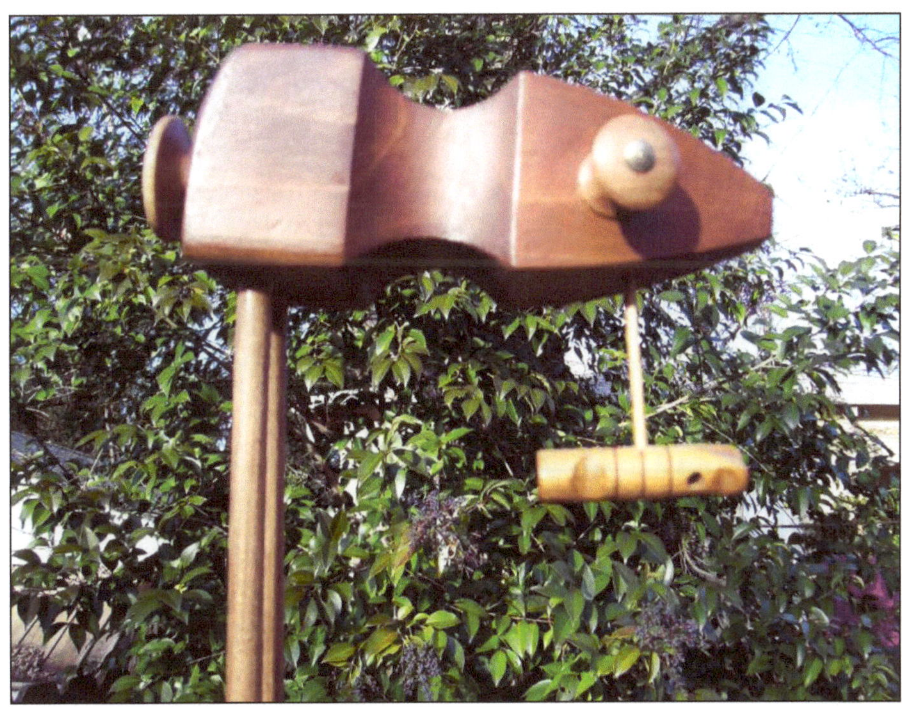

Mayan Bird of Paradise, carved wood and found objects, 24" x 16" including base (at left, and close-ups above)

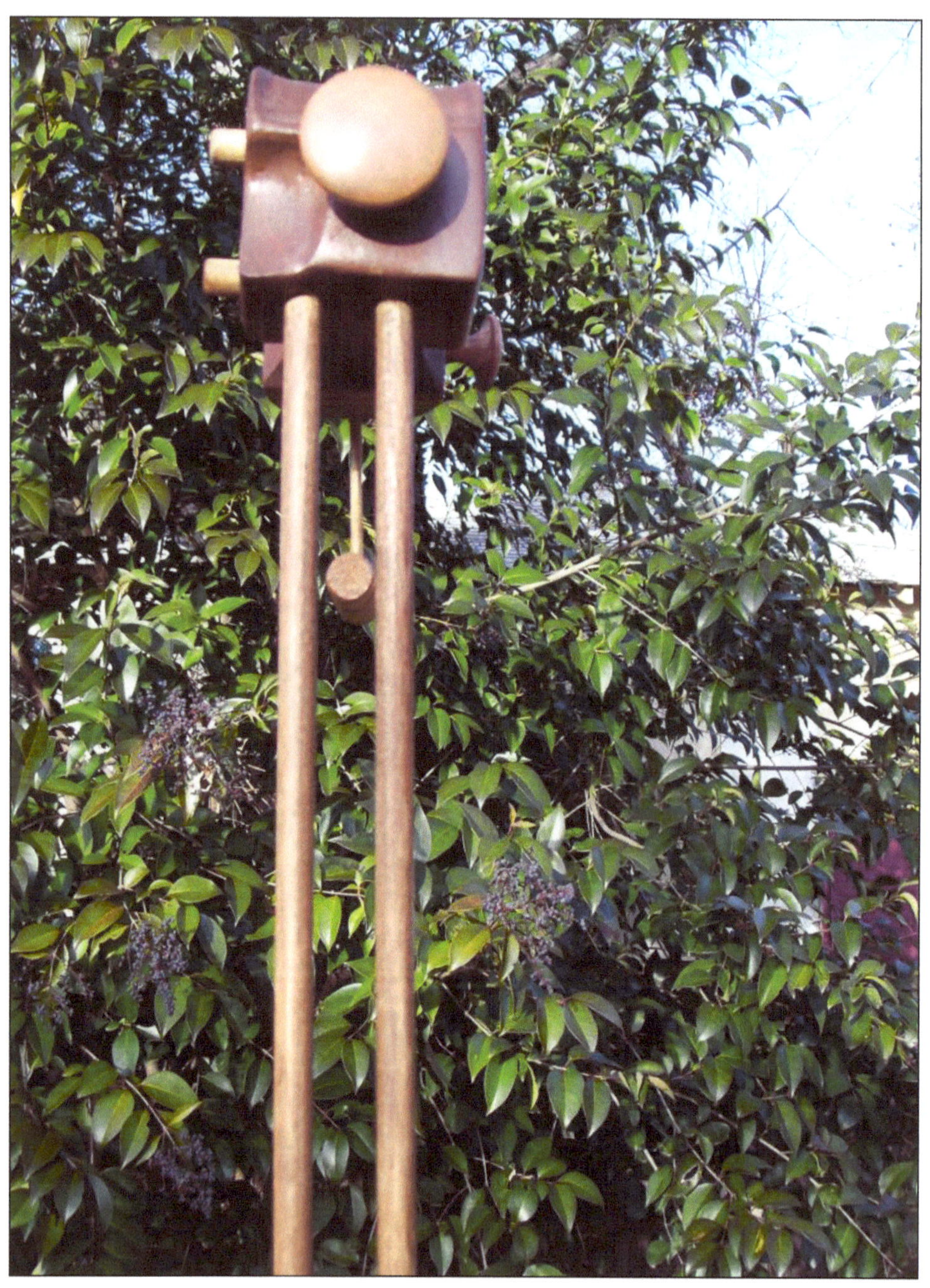

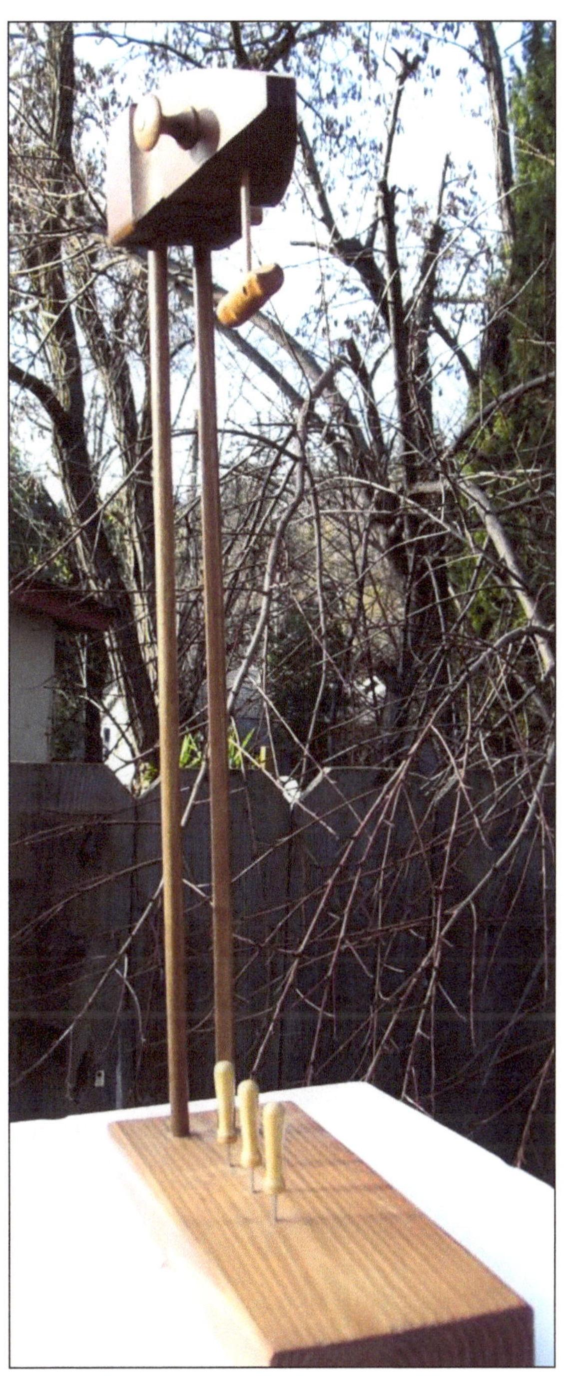

Mayan Bird of Paradise, carved wood and found objects, 24" x 16" including base (at left, and above)

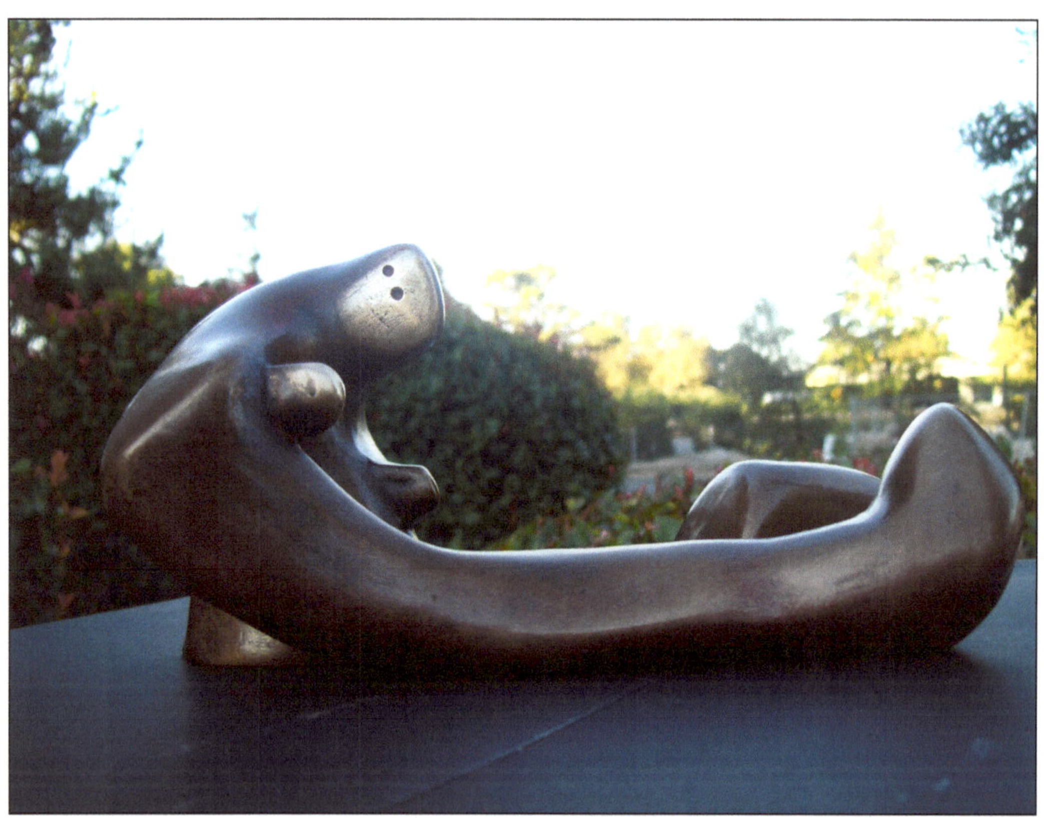

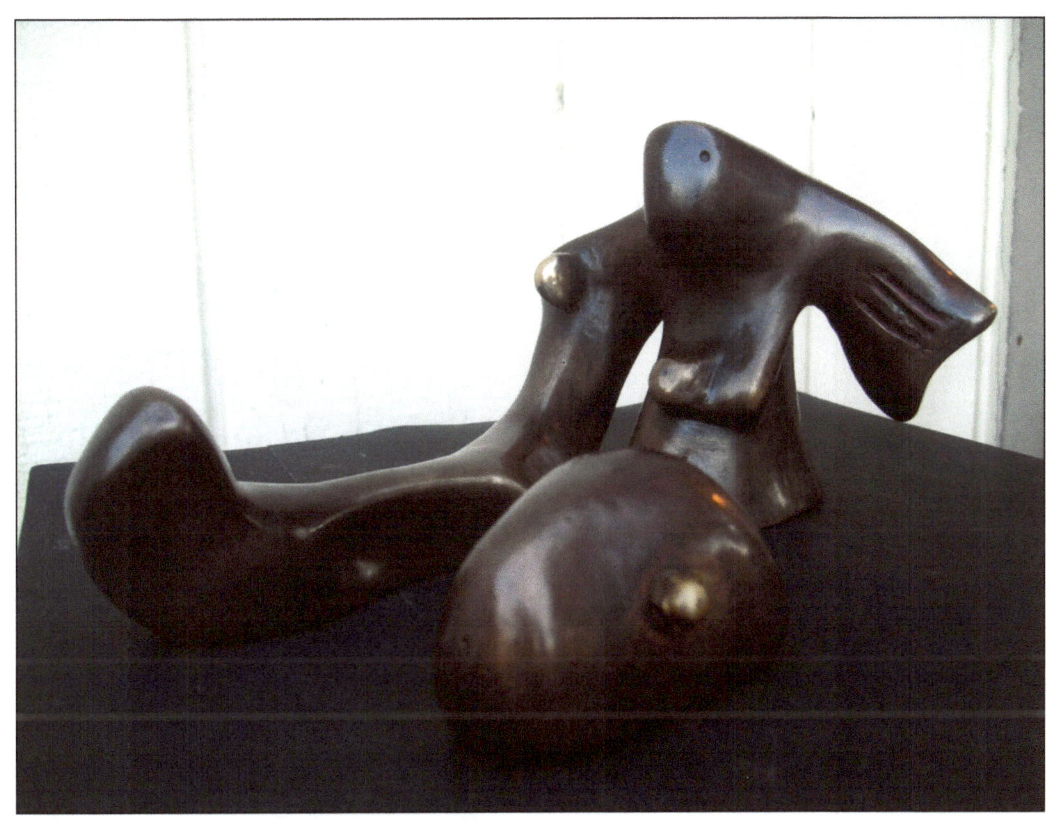

Virago Pursuing Man, bronze (at left, and above)

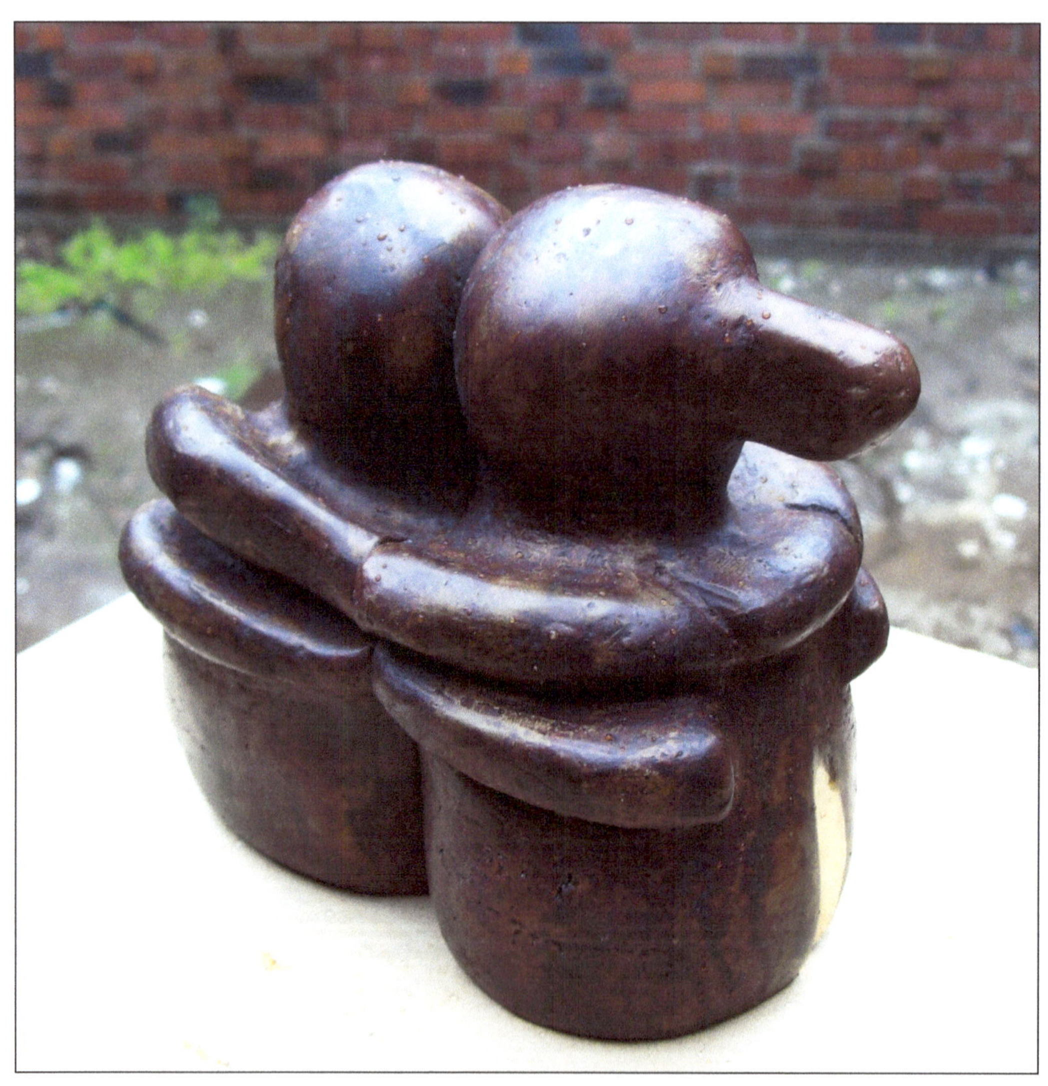

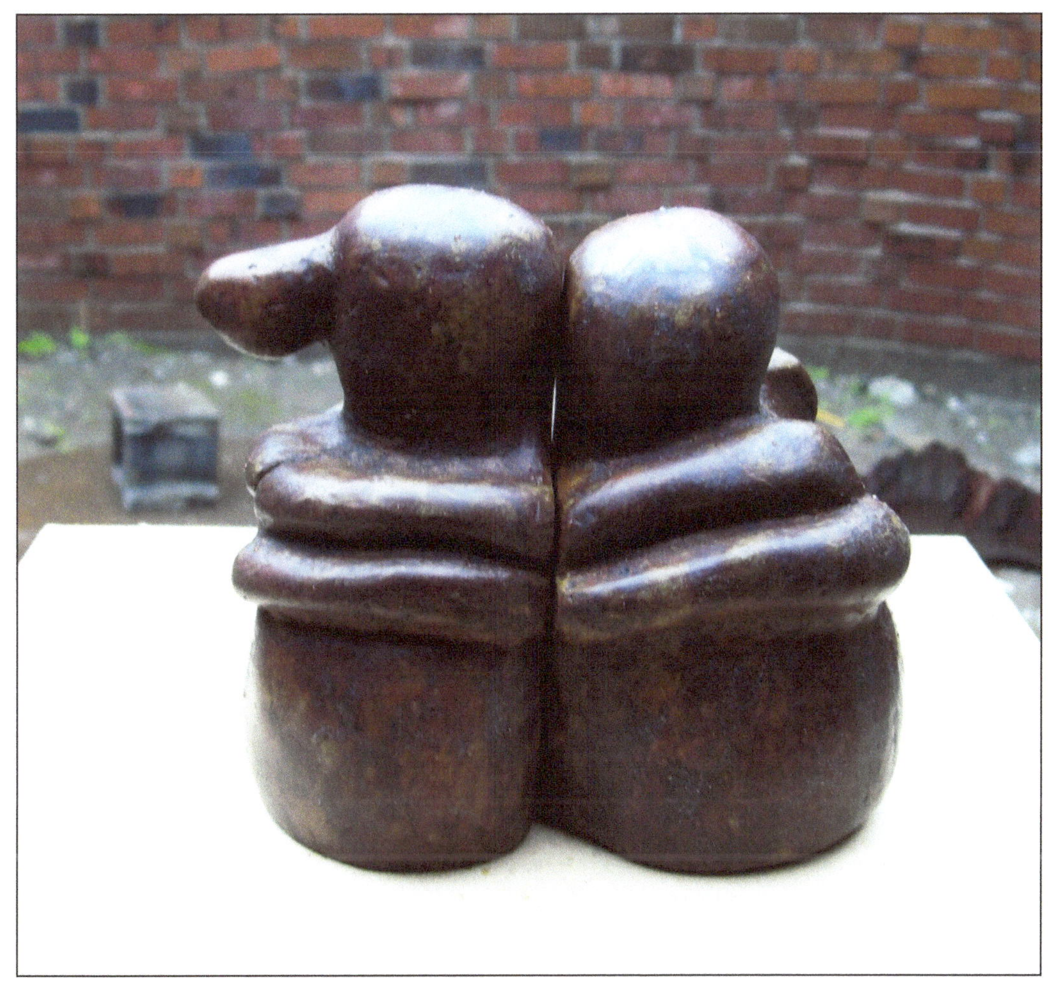

The First Kiss: Homage to Britt-Marie Olofsson-Harris, bronze (at left, and above)

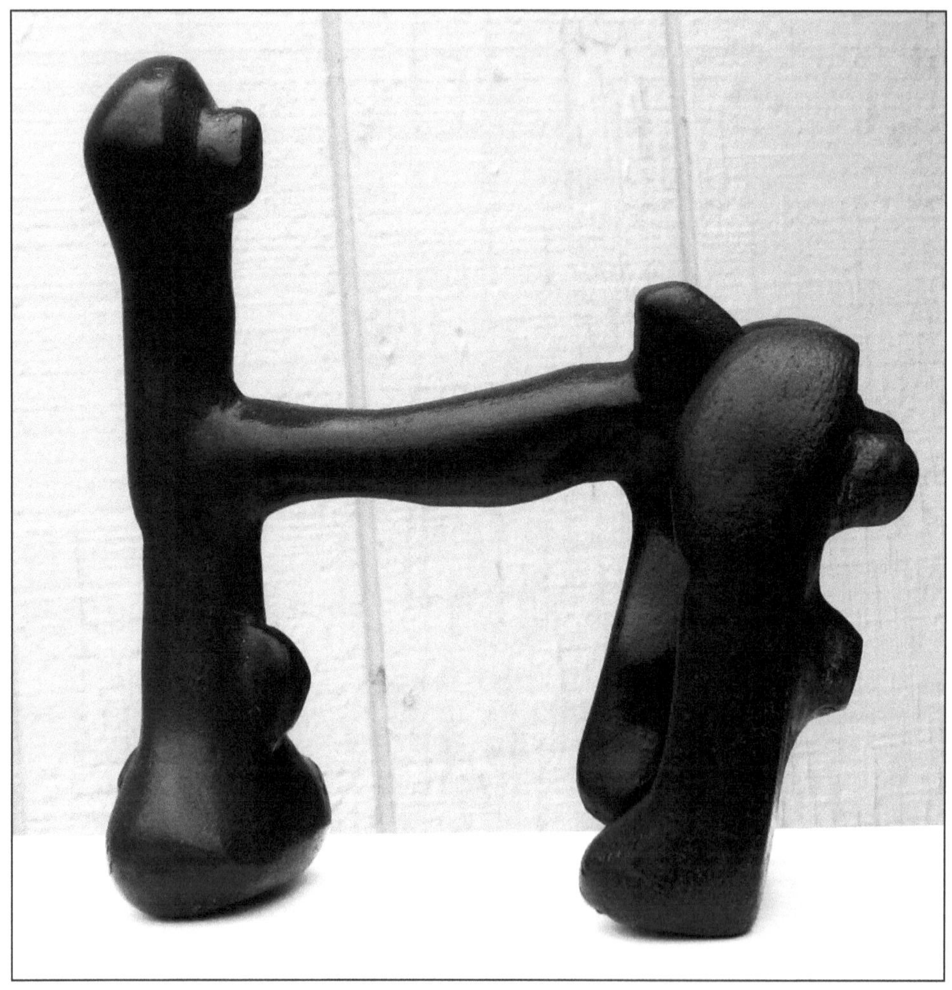

The Struggle, clay model for bronze. Fiberglass tape and bondo (above, and at right)

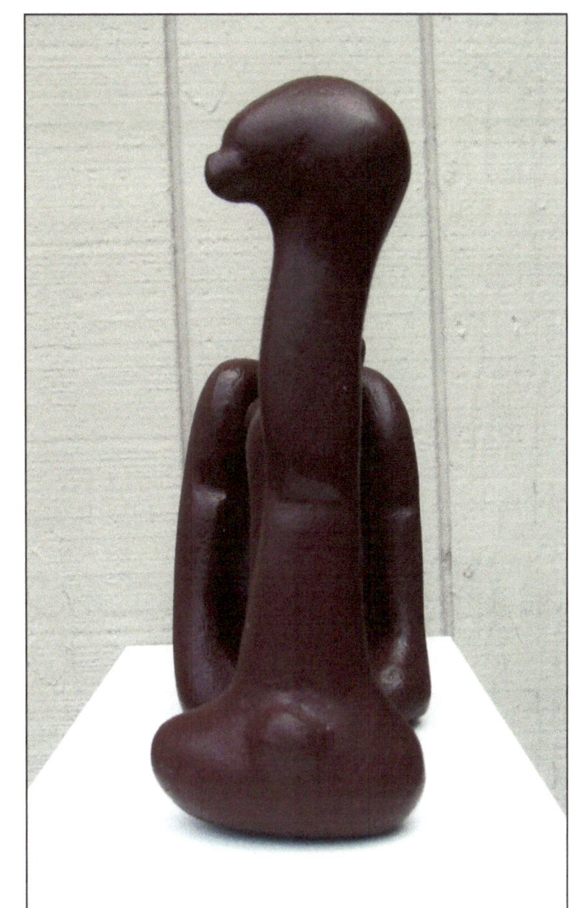

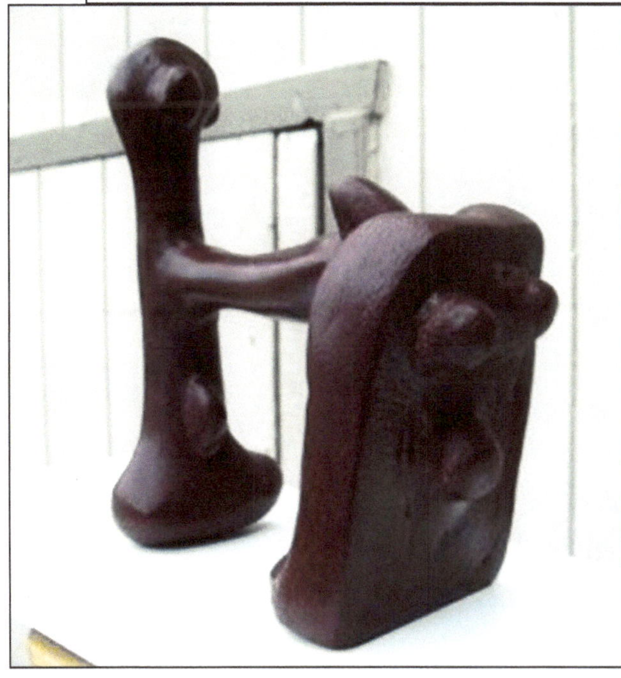

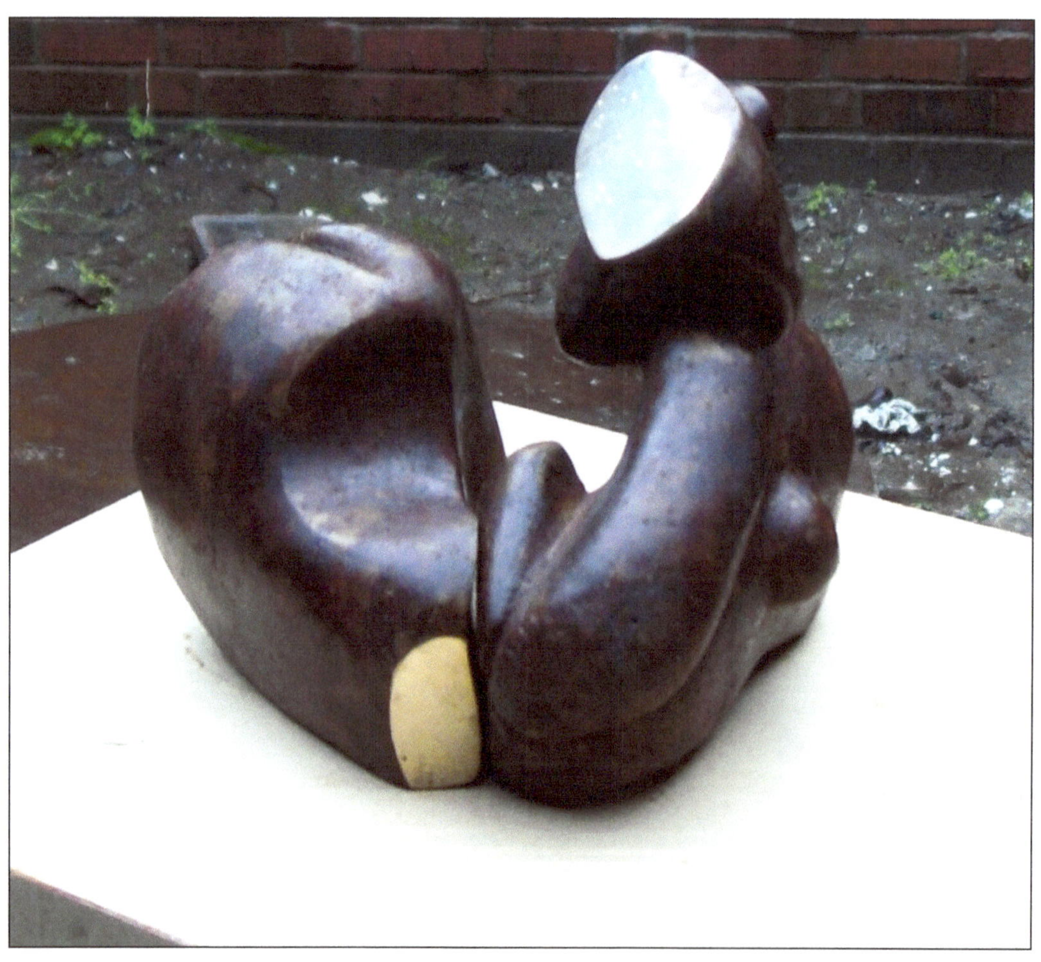

Primal Scream, bronze (above, and at right)

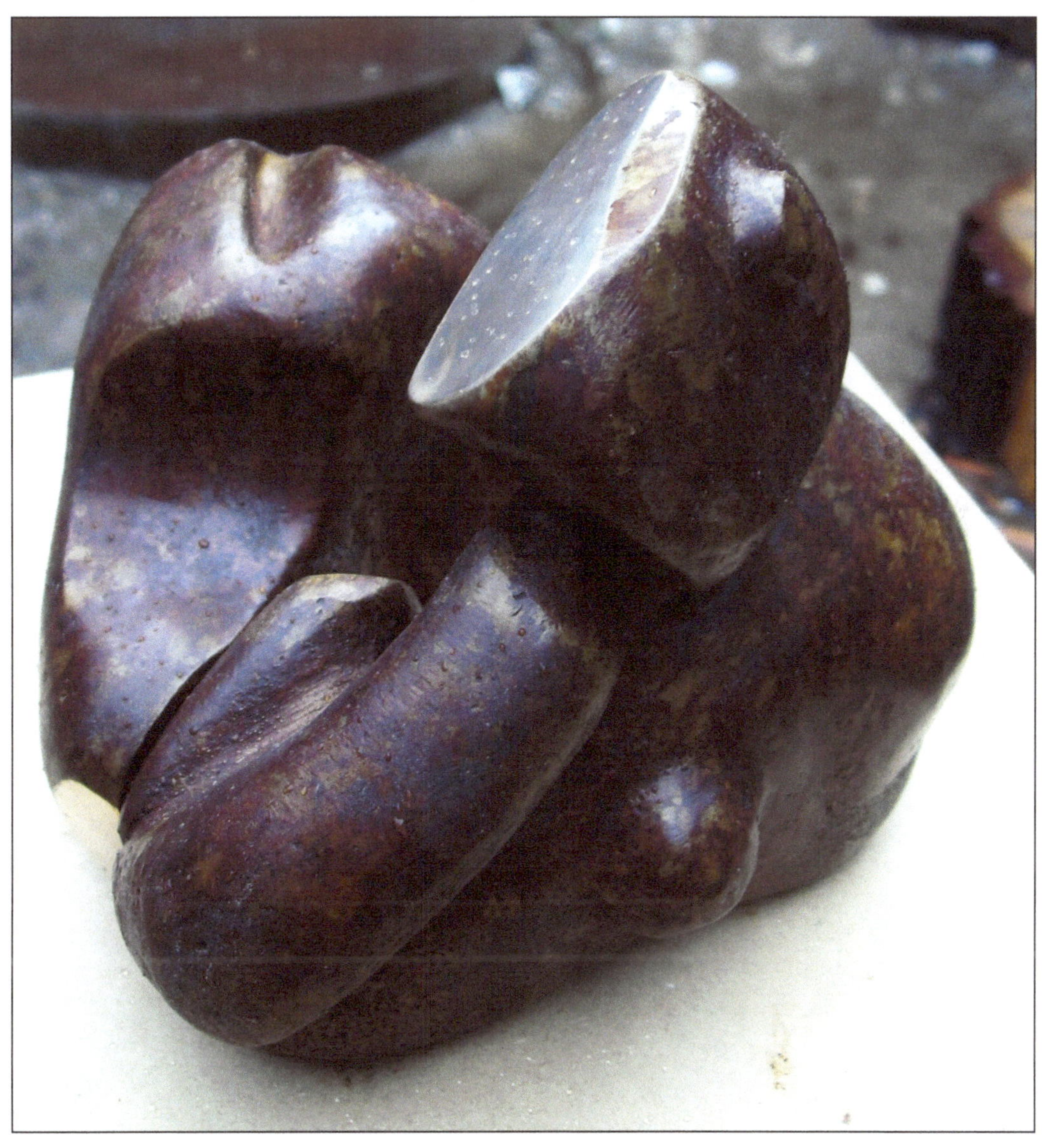

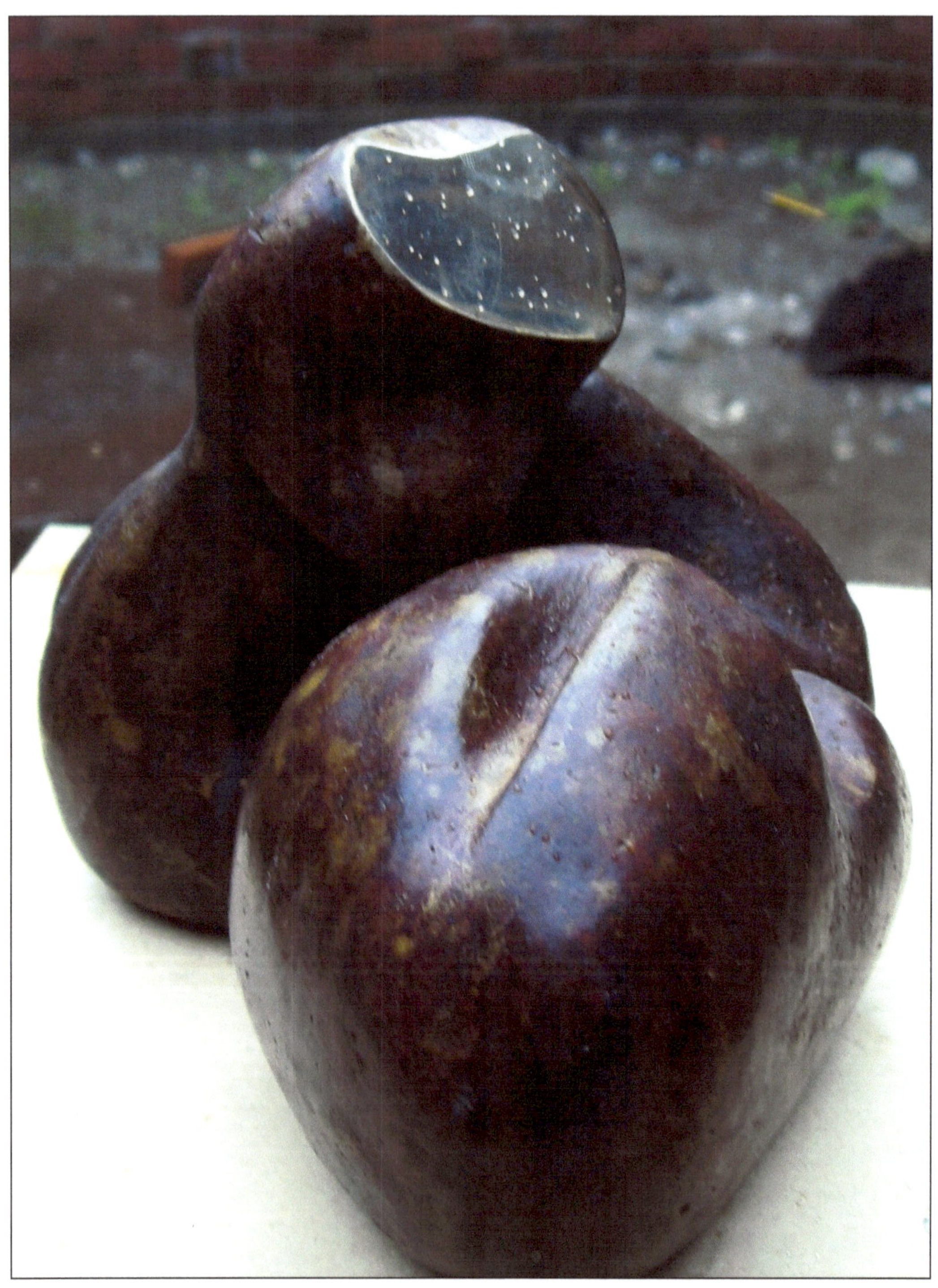

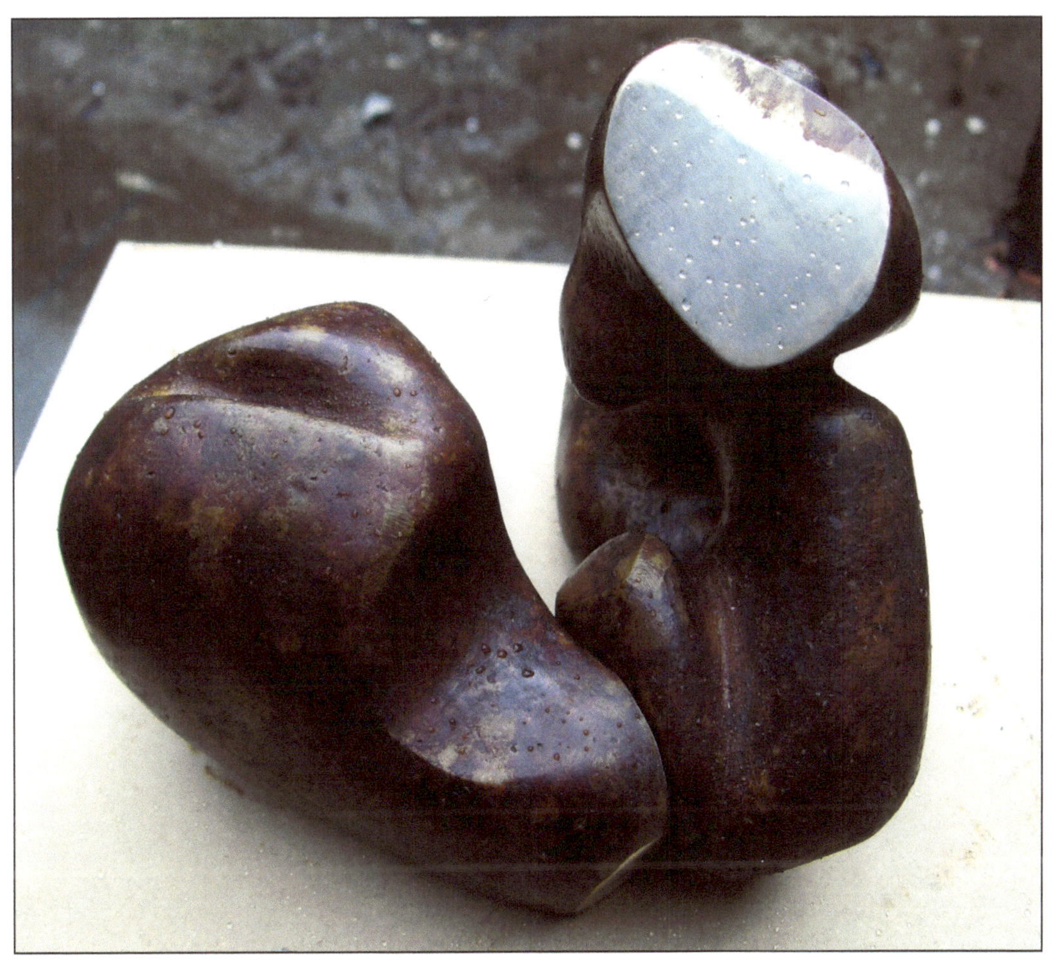

Primal Scream, bronze (above, and at left)

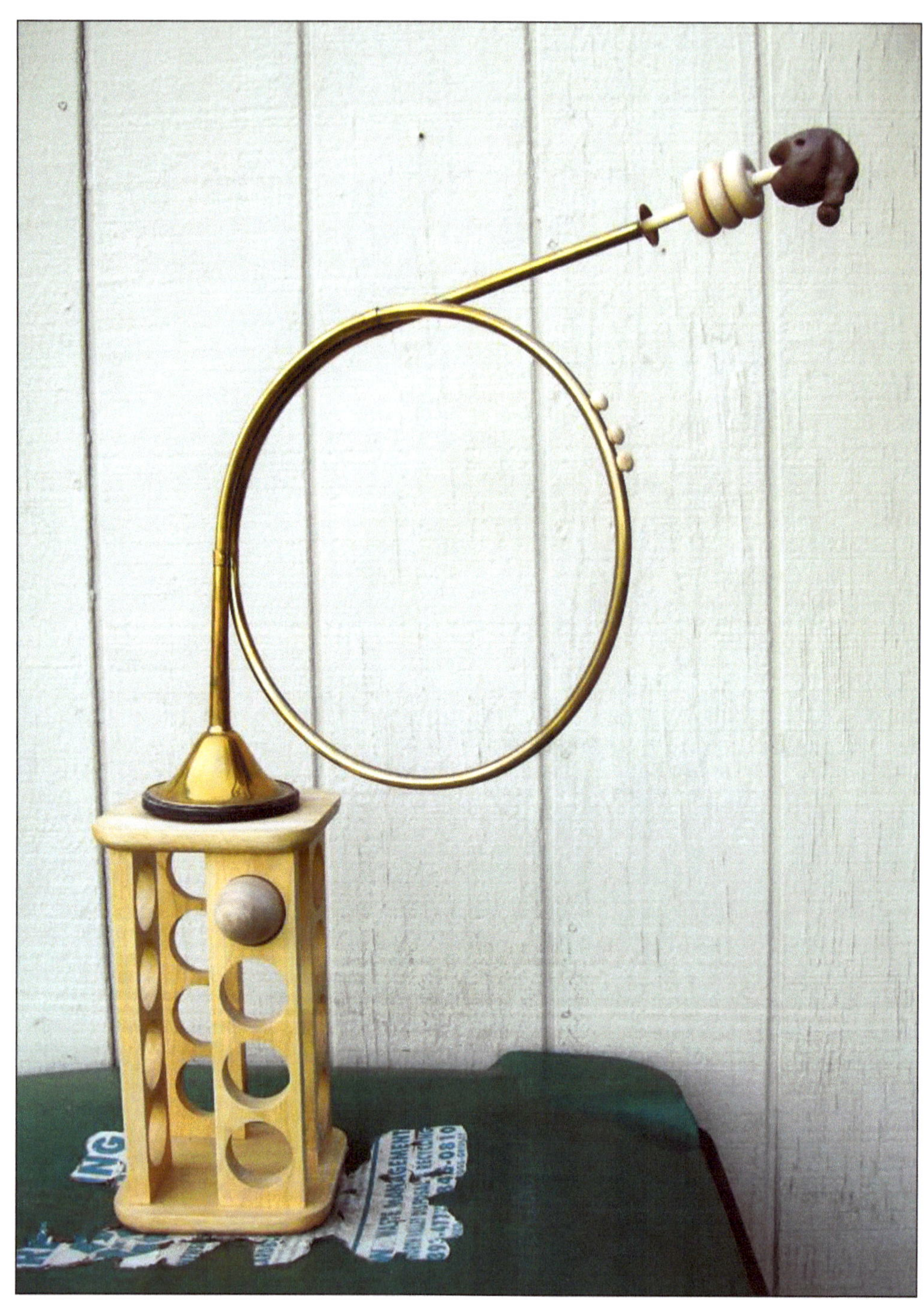

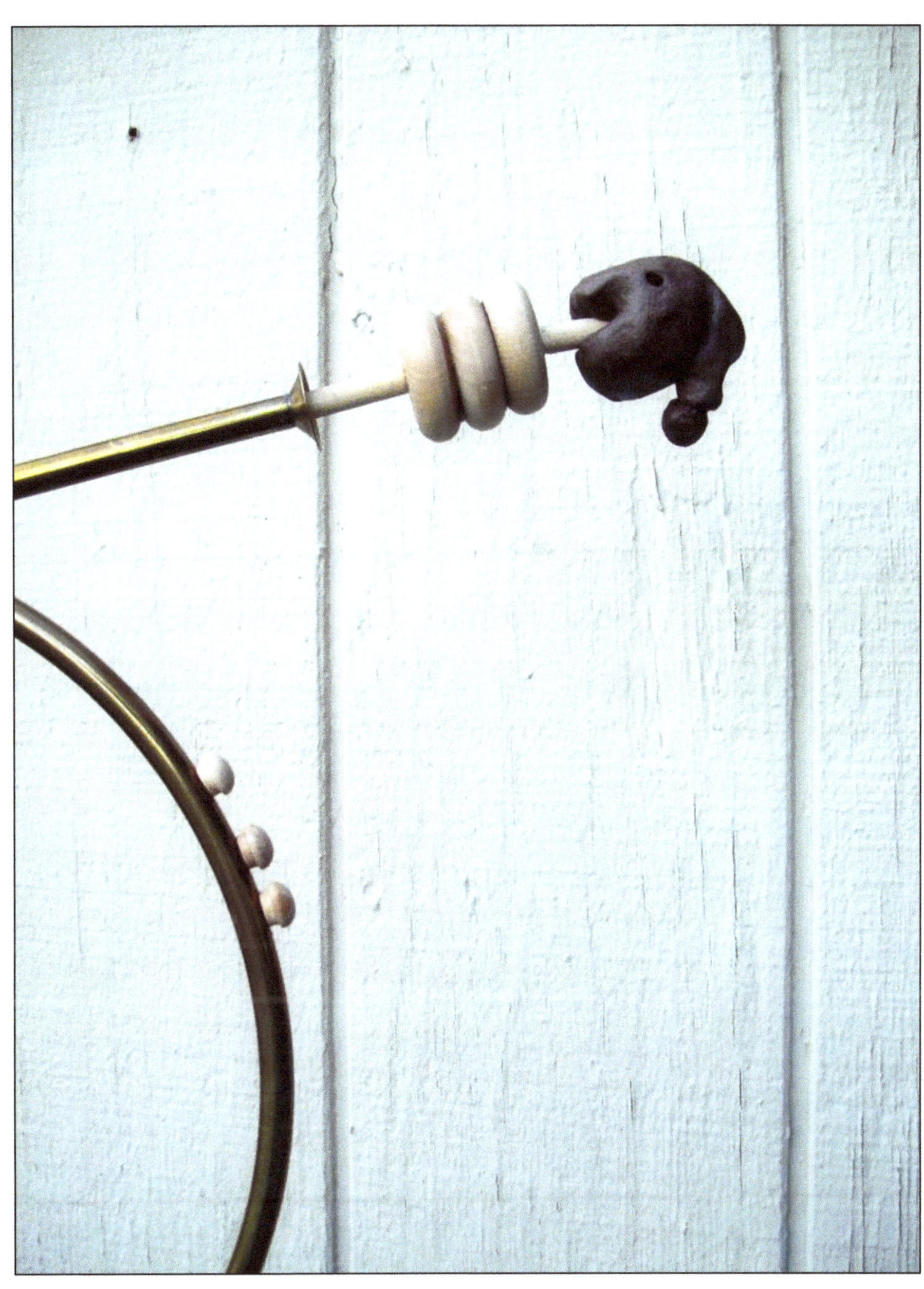

Tutu - Homage to Miles Davis, brass, found objects, and fiberglass (at left, and above)

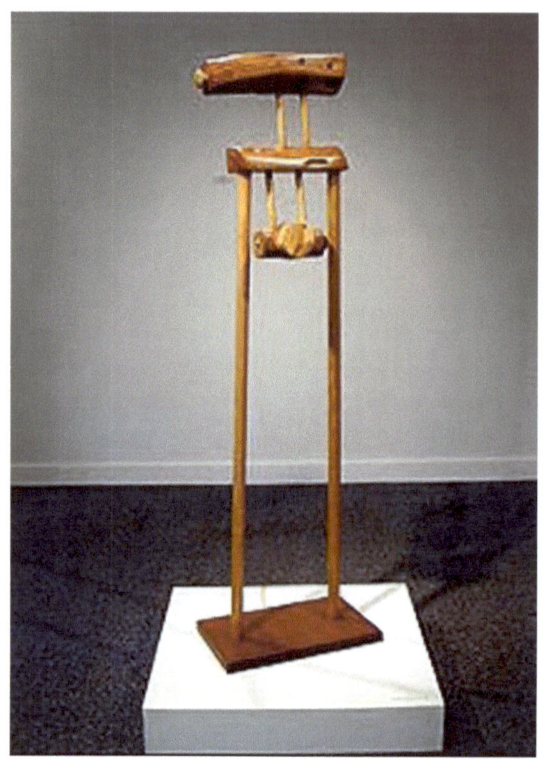

Screaming Mother and Child, carved and constructed wood, 5 ft. 6" tall

www.ingramcontent.com/pod-product-compliance
Lightning Source LLC
LaVergne TN
LVHW070137110826
845147LV00002B/273
* 9 7 8 0 9 8 2 5 7 0 4 1 8 *